SPIRIT BODY HEALING

*Using Your Mind's Eye
to Unlock the Medicine Within*

Michael Samuels, M.D.
Mary Rockwood Lane, R.N., Ph.D.

RESOURCE *Publications* • Eugene, Oregon

Resource Publications
A division of Wipf and Stock Publishers
199 W 8th Ave, Suite 3
Eugene, OR 97401

Spirit Body Healing
Using Your Mind's Eye to Unlock the Medicine Within
By Samuels, Michael, MD and Lane, Mary Rockwood, RN, PhD
Copyright©2000 by Samuels, Michael, MD
ISBN 13: 978-1-61097-165-2
Publication date 12/17/2010
Previously published by John Wiley & Sons, Inc., 2000

*Michael: To Mary Rockwood Lane in deep thanks
for bringing me this spirit-lifting project*

*Mary: To my family, Tim, Anneliese, David,
and Frankie for their support and love*

Contents

Preface by Mary Rockwood Lane	xi
The Research Study	*xii*
Moving from Darkness to Transcendence	*xiv*
Teachings from the Edge	*xv*
Acknowledgments	xvii
Introduction: The First Path for People to Heal with Spirit by Michael Samuels	1
Use Spirit Body Healing to Heal Your Whole Life	*2*
Help Your Inner Healer	*2*
PART ONE: UNDERSTANDING SPIRIT BODY HEALING	5
Chapter 1. The Experience of Spirit Body Healing	7
Spirit Body Healing to Help You Change Your Life	*10*
Use This Book to Heal	*11*
You Know the Ending Before You Start, So Start the Process with Faith	*13*

CONTENTS

Use Guided Imagery	*14*
Begin to Heal Now	*19*

Chapter 2. The Process of Spirit Body Healing   21

The Eight Spirals of Spirit Body Healing	*22*
Restory Your Life	*24*
Invite a Peak Spiritual Experience to Come to You	*25*

Chapter 3. How Spirit Body Healing Works:
Unlocking the Medicine Within   27

The Spiritual Experience Is Perceived as Imagery	*28*
Longevity and the Spirit	*32*

PART TWO: THE EIGHT STEPS OF SPIRIT BODY HEALING   35

Chapter 4. Step One: Go into Your Own Pain
and Darkness   37

Pain is the Doorway to Spirit Body Healing	*39*
Move from Pain to Beauty	*41*
Use Books As Tools to Start Your Journey	*43*
Turn Fear into Compassion	*46*
Pain Deepens to Darkness	*46*
Remember Things Past	*49*
Extract Your Pain	*49*
Reflections on Pain and Darkness	*50*
Use Guided Imagery	*52*

Chapter 5. Step Two: Go Elsewhere   59

Restory Your Own Life	*61*
The Pause Invites You	*62*
Reclaim Your Dreamer Within	*63*

Go Inward into Your Heart	*64*
The Trigger Event Invites You	*66*
Reflections on Going Elsewhere	*70*
Use Guided Imagery	*72*

Chapter 6. Step Three: Find Your Own Turning Point   77

Be Creative	*80*
Open Your Mind to Something New	*82*
Reflections from the Turning Point:	
Follow Your Passion to Your Turning Point	*95*
Use Guided Imagery	*96*

Chapter 7. Step Four: Slip through the Veil   99

Slip into Enchantment	*100*
Feel the Spaciousness Inside	*101*
Go into Mystical Enchantment	*102*
Breathe in Oneness	*106*
Reflections on Going through the Veil:	
Merge with a Greater Power	*106*
Use Guided Imagery	*107*

Chapter 8. Step Five: Know the Truth and Trust the Process   111

Know It's the Truth	*112*
Reflections on Knowing the Truth and	
Trusting the Process	*116*
Use Guided Imagery	*119*

Chapter 9. Step Six: Embody Your Spirit   123

You Can Embody Spirit	*127*
Allow Spirit to Come into You from the Earth	*130*

CONTENTS

Reflections on the Embodiment of Spirit   *132*
Use Guided Imagery   *134*

Chapter 10. Step Seven: Feel the Healing Energy of Love and Compassion   137

Feel Compassion and Healing Energy   *140*
Use Humor to Release Healing Energy   *143*
Feel Compassion for Yourself   *146*
Reflections on Healing Energy and Compassion:
    Release Judgment and See with Compassion   *146*
Use Guided Imagery   *147*

Chapter 11. Step Eight: Experience Transcendence   151

See Yourself As Surrounded by God and the Angels   *153*
Share Your Love   *154*
Illuminosity: Be within the Light   *154*
Move from Healing Illness to Healing the Earth   *167*
Reflections on Transcendence   *169*
Use Guided Imagery   *170*

PART THREE: THE SPIRIT BODY HEALING METHOD   179

Chapter 12. The Prescription for Spirit Body Healing   181

Starbursts within the Stories Reveal Wisdom   *181*
Step One: Go into Your Own Pain and Darkness   *182*
Step Two: Go Elsewhere   *185*
Step Three: Find Your Own Turning Point   *189*
Step Four: Slip through the Veil   *196*
Step Five: Know the Truth and Trust the Process   *198*
Step Six: Embody Your Own Spirit   *201*

*Step Seven: Feel the Healing Energy of Love
   and Compassion*   *204*
Step Eight: Experience Transcendence   *207*

Chapter 13. The Teachings from the Edge   215

*Raise the Storyteller to the Level of the
   Wisdom Keeper*   *215*
Learn the Teachings from the Edge   *215*

Epilogue: I Close My Eyes in the Darkness   219

Recommended Reading   223

References   235

Resources   245

Index   247

Preface
by Mary Rockwood Lane

Commit to it and the universe will make it happen."

—Goethe

Years ago, when I was in the deepest depression and in my greatest moment of despair, I began to paint. The act of painting was so powerful, it changed my life. No one had ever told me I could take the pain and the darkness of my life—my sadness, my fears—and use them creatively to heal myself.

Everywhere I had looked before, it seemed as though I had been in relationship with a form of healing that was disjointed from my life. The different strategies did not support me in the way I needed them to. It was not until I threw myself into my artistic work that I actually began to heal. My whole life became enmeshed in the healing process and emerged into this healing journey. I became totally involved with it. That was what I needed because I had previously been totally involved with my depression every moment of my day. I now need healing in every moment, as well. With painting, I felt a powerful healing. I experienced a transformation; I became empowered. I even saw my own spirit illuminated.

This experience filled me with a desire to reach out to other people. Because I was a nurse and creativity had healed me, I believed that bringing creativity into the health-care system would heal others. I wanted to create an opportunity for others to be invited to heal themselves in this way.

I realized that no one would suggest bringing artists and the arts into the hospital. I needed to do that on my own, so I created a program bringing artists and the arts into the practice of healing. I went to the College of Nursing at the University of Florida and began a doctoral program and a research study on how creativity heals. This research provided a framework and focus that helped me create a model for implementing art in the hospital.

The research study for my Ph.D. in nursing is the research that *Spirit Body Healing* is based on. I completed the research while immersed in the Arts in Medicine program that was helping hundreds of people. In my study, I started out by looking at how art heals, how creativity heals. To my great surprise, I found that the spirit heals.

The Research Study

Spirit Body Healing is based on my research study on how the spirit heals, conducted at Shands Hospital from 1992 to 1999 at the University of Florida. My study was sponsored and partially funded by the university's College of Medicine. I took detailed interviews of people who had been through life crises or had healed themselves of life-threatening illnesses and I analyzed their stories to elucidate the themes and essences of how the healing occurred.

Spirit Body Healing is the first book on spiritual healing to come from a research study in a major university health-care center. It is the first book based on research on healing with the spirit, which has been peer reviewed, analyzed, and evaluated. The study this book is based on was a seven-year research project. From its inception, it was guided by academic physicians and nurses on faculty at the University of Florida—

a mainstream medical facility, not an alternative university that customarily does research on mind-body processes.

The professors of medicine and nursing and the physicians and nurses on the hospital staff helped make the study hold to accepted methods. Even though *Spirit Body Healing* is about the spirit, this material came from the scientific method and is deeply rooted in the mainstream medical system.

The research was a phenomenological study using the technique of *hermeneutic aesthetic inquiry* in which a lived experience of healing is examined. The hermeneutic method is a qualitative health-research technique that involves examining the lived experience of a person through detailed interviews. The method focuses on the description of thoughts, feelings, body sensations, and the story of the actual event. The researcher listens to the description of lived experience rather than to the person's theories or analysis of what happened to him. The researcher then elucidates the themes that come from the actual experiences. *Aesthetic inquiry* involves the use of aesthetic materials such as art, video, and photographs as part of data collection, in addition to interviews.

A *phenomenological study* involves finding the essences of what you are looking at; it is about opening your mind to all possibilities without judgment and about looking deeper. The phenomenological technique is not unusual in health-care research. It is an excellent way of studying the evanescent, the mysterious, the places where numbers and statistics cannot fully inform us about what is happening. It is used with cancer patients, in neonatal units, in all aspects of health-care research.

In the search for the truth, the scientific method led us to spirit. This is a book about how you can use this groundbreaking research to allow your spirit to heal.

PREFACE

Moving from Darkness to Transcendence

In analyzing the interviews, I made an important discovery. Over and over again, people said that they went to a place inside themselves where they actually experienced a shift of consciousness. This shift allowed them to see their whole lives in a new way. When the shift in point of view occurred, the life healing began.

Although the experiences were different for each person, the underlying themes were the same. Each person went from a place of profound darkness, fear, or illness to a place where they experienced luminosity: After healing, they described feeling intensely alive and transformed. Each person described a transcendent way of being; each person's spirit became awakened, visible, and illuminated. After going inward, the person glimpses darkness and light, feels healing energy, feels or sees her or his spirit, and feels or sees this spirit heal the body. The person's body feelings were concrete and were most often described as illumination or luminosity. In the study, we called this experience "illuminosity." Each person had a different experience of transcendence, but for all of them, the experience of transcendence was a recognizable phenomenon that was the main feature of their physical and psychological healing.

The research consistently revealed eight themes in each story:

1. Pain and darkness
2. Going elsewhere
3. Being creative at a turning point
4. Slipping through the veil
5. Knowing the truth and trusting the process
6. Embodying spirit
7. Feeling healing energy and compassion
8. Transcendence

We discuss each theme in its own chapter. You will be able to understand the themes by reading the stories of our participants and seeing through their eyes.

While Michael Samuels and I wrote a previous book, *Creative Healing*, I showed him my research from the university study. I realized that his work with self-help medicine and mind-body healing—and his experience with his patients in his own practice—would allow us to collaborate powerfully to make my study available to people outside of the medical establishment. We worked on the research for several years to devise a method that would turn my study into a prescription for patients. We then interviewed more patients and presented the material to professional conferences for review and criticism. The material grew and deepened, as the stories told us more each time we read them. That is how *Spirit Body Healing* was born.

Teachings from the Edge

The people we interviewed who were in crises or very ill were great teachers. For us, they became our contemporary spiritual teachers. They are at the threshold, at the edge, closest to God. People who are very ill are closer to the spirit world as they face death. In a sense, they speak to you from the other side because a part of them is already there. You can see their grace.

Their teachings are a great gift. Why wait in our lives until we hit the wall—whatever that is for each of us? We can learn from people who are ill or in crises and heal before we experience such suffering. For instance, I interviewed a dancer who told me this story:

> One day, in a bone-marrow transplant ward, a little girl with leukemia dances as an angel. She puts on cloth wings, a

flowing silk dress. She puts a flowing scarf over her bald head. She spins and whirls and spins and whirls. I see the girl's spirit dance, and the little girl's mother does, too. For a moment, the little girl has transcended her physical form. She moves in a way that gives her powerful freedom. She can feel her spirit not contained by her body anymore, not trapped in the limitation of her own little body. Her spirit fills the whole room with the spirit of the dance. It happened in an instant, her experience of transcendence. I saw it and felt it, and my spirit was free, too.

As you practice Spirit Body Healing, it will lead you to transcendence. It will lead you to healing energy; it will lead you to see angels, God. It will lead you to feel healing energy and forgiveness. The promise of the book is that if you embody these lived experiences of healing, you will have the opportunity in your own life for your spirit to blossom and become illuminated. As we heal, we have the opportunity for grace.

Acknowledgments

We would both like to thank our teachers from the edge, all the children, women, and men, who shared their moving stories of courage and healing with us and then with you. The extraordinary beauty of each of their spirits radiates to us across time and space.

We would both like to thank our families for support during this long project. We would like to thank Elaine Markson, our agent, for continuing to be a beacon of light guiding our work. We thank Tom Miller, our editor, for a heartfelt, hardworking, edit.

Mary would like to thank the faculty of University of Florida College of Nursing for their support of the research that made *Spirit Body Healing* possible: her committee, Sally Hutchinson, Carol Reed Ash, Sandra Seymore, Jerry Cutler, and John Graham Pole. Max Van Manen for his teaching and his passionate sharing of his method, and Jean Watson for teaching of support of spirit in nursing. She would also like to thank her friend Jan Poser for her spiritual wisdom.

Introduction

The First Path for People to Heal with Spirit

by Michael Samuels

I am powerfully affected by the results of Mary's Spirit Body Healing study. I have been a physician taking care of cancer patients and patients with life-threatening illness for twenty-five years. I have used relaxation, guided imagery, and meditation, and these mind-body techniques have helped my patients immensely. When I established Art as a Healing Force in 1990, I incorporated art into my practice and found creativity to be a powerful healing tool, too. My deep interest in art and healing led me to meet Mary Rockwood Lane, and we started working together on our first collaboration, *Creative Healing*.

When I read her research study, I knew it was important. This was the first time I had seen a framework for what I had seen happening with my patients over the years. Her study showed for the first time the steps my patients had taken when they had healed themselves with spirit. I knew this study was a milestone in mind-body medicine, and I believe that it will set the parameters for mind-body healing for years. This work allows us to understand what is happening when a person heals him- or herself with spirit, and more important, it allows us to help patients do it with intent. Patients can follow the path and heal with spirit.

Use Spirit Body Healing to Heal Your Whole Life

In all my years with spirit-mind-body medicine, I have never seen as powerful a healing technique as the spirit body technique. The stories of the people in this study are truly remarkable. The people have healed themselves of life-threatening illnesses, including cancer, heart disease, and severe depressions. More than that, they have gone beyond physical healing and have healed their whole lives. The lives they now lead are in service—full of meaning, rich and satisfying. They have found out who they are and are now helping others and doing work to heal their neighborhoods and the earth.

This technique is unique to healing as I know it. Not only does it heal the illness, but it also changes people's lives so that they are in harmony with the Earth. They show a wonderful, lively sense of enthusiasm and a desire to share the experience with others. For our patients, Spirit Body Healing is almost like a religious conversion or an experience of cosmic consciousness. Spirit Body Healing not only heals the body and cures the illness, but it also produces the experience of seeing the spirit, angels, and God—a peak experience in the world's great religions. It is the most remarkable experience I have had in my years of mind-body healing.

Help Your Inner Healer

My whole career as a physician has been dedicated to mind-body healing technology and self-care medicine. My previous books have basically melded self-help and mind-body medicine to produce a way people can take charge of their lives and help their inner healer function optimally. When patients can optimize their blood flow and their immune system and can make their attitude hopeful and positive, powerful healing takes place. Like many physicians working with mind-body techniques, I have seen many of my patients get well when all predictions were dire.

In *Spirit Body Healing*, we have created a way each of us can make the spirit-body connection deeper and more real. We have taken the experiences in the research and made them into steps that take the spirit and illuminate it, thereby allowing it to change the body and help heal physical illness. This process makes the spirit and body one, the embodiment of spirit. This technique takes the spirit and makes it physical, allowing it to be seen and felt as body sensations, feelings, inner voices, and inner visions.

During most of my life as a physician, my basic mind-body technique has been guided imagery. My 1975 book *Seeing with the Mind's Eye* was the first book published on guided imagery. It helped people use their minds' eyes to unlock the medicine within. Guided imagery brings to light the healing images that are within each of us so they can help us heal. This technique allows your body's knowledge of how to optimize its healing systems work for you to heal you. In *Spirit Body Healing*, Mary and I have taken proven guided-imagery techniques and applied them to the research, creating a prescriptive method. We have built a series of graded exercises, activities, and guided-imagery exercises that allow you to experience the same transcendence and spirit healing Mary saw in her study.

In each chapter, we tell you a series of stories, we go on to see what the stories mean in a reflection, and then we offer exercises in guided imagery, so that you can have the experience.

Mary and I both believe that Spirit Body Healing is a revolutionary next act, a quantum leap in mind-body healing, which brings us to a different dimension in health care. As a physician and as a nurse, we see it as a new way of knowing about spirit and healing.

We are only beginning to heal in this dimension. In this new millennium, we will heal on the energy spirit level. We will have a profound awareness of our lives before birth and after death. We will become eternal awakened beings, aware of our passage through life and death. As we evolve in consciousness, we will develop an awareness of being an eternal spiritual being, which will be our new perspective.

In the beginning, we were creatures of the body, then the mind, now the spirit. Spirit Body Healing uses this knowledge to heal now.

Part One

Understanding Spirit Body Healing

CHAPTER 1

The Experience of Spirit Body Healing

The Face of God in a Butterfly Swarm

She had Hodgkin's lymphoma. She was thirty years old and had spent most of her twenties fighting cancer. She told us this story:

> This is my third recurrence of Hodgkin's. When I got the news, I became very depressed. The tumor is now below my diaphragm, and the doctor told me that this means my prognosis is poor. Last week I was walking in the park near my home. I was walking and crying. It seemed to me there was no hope anymore. I had been up all night, and I was exhausted. All I thought about was dying. I thought about my friends. I thought about what I had missed and what I would miss. My mind said to myself over and over again, "I have never married, I do not have children. I have never made a career. I have been in and out of hospitals all my adult life." I walked and I could not get my mind off my situation. I felt so sorry for myself, it seemed to me that my life was over

and I had not done anything, I had not found what I was looking for. I yearned for meaning, for comfort. My life was so hard.

It was dawn. The sun had not yet risen. This park was one of my favorite places on Earth. It was a place where migrating monarch butterflies came to rest. I had never seen the butterflies. The migration took place only one week a year, and I was never there at that time. I had always been in the hospital. The park was beautiful, and the trees the butterflies nested in were always there even if the butterflies were not. As I walked, I looked around me. The sun was coming up, casting long beams of light towards me across the dark forest. As I saw them I forgot about my illness. I was taken elsewhere. The beams looked to me as if they were coming from heaven. They were like God's light.

Then I saw something extraordinary. Hundreds of butterflies were swarming. I said to myself, this must be the time of the migration. The swarm came towards me and stopped in the place where the sunbeams emerged from one point. The rising sun made the beams come out of a perfect circle like a halo. Then the butterfly swarm seemed to stop moving. It formed a shape like a face. It was as if my eyes crossed and something changed. The world cracked and sizzled. I was deep in another place. It was only a moment, a flash.

Then I knew, the face I saw was the face of God. He was in the place the butterflies had been. He was glimmering, a halo of light was around him. He was the most beautiful sight I had ever seen. Time stood still. It was as if he had always been there. It was as if I had always been there. He spoke to me: "There is nothing to fear. I love you. I have always loved you. I will be with you always." He lifted his arms as if he was blessing me. Light came out of his hands and came to me. A beam of light came into my heart and I prayed to him. I prayed on that beam: "Thank you. May I have peace. May your blessing come to me and may whatever is supposed to happen, happen." Tears came down my face. I knew suddenly that with my bald head and with my tears I was as beautiful as any other woman throughout time who had ever seen a spiritual vision. I felt my beauty. A prayer came back to me on the beam of light and came into my heart. It was his blessing and everlasting love.

I looked again and he was gone. The butterflies were back. I was tingling, full of energy. The butterfly swarm had moved away from the light. It was now in a shadow in the forest. I now could see the butterflies clearly. My eyes opened wide and I looked around me. There were thousands of butterflies. They were lit up in the light beams, moving like pure energy. I could see, too, that some of the butterflies were now dead. They still held onto the branches and trembled in the soft breeze. It was like they were speaking to me, too. I wondered. Did they come to this grove to mate and die like the salmon come to rivers? I felt like they had come to the grove to speak to me today. In their beauty I could see that their death was natural, beautiful, and even calm.

And in that moment, I knew that my death was not something I needed to fear any more. The butterflies were beautiful beyond meaning, and in that moment, I was, too. I knew that the spirit of God had come to me and spoken to me. Whether it was him or butterflies or a vision did not matter to me then. God spoke to me about love, the butterflies spoke to me about death. They were one voice, the voice of my spirit. I knew I was now deeply different, maybe I would never be the same again. I felt deep love and peace come over me, surround me. I saw my own beauty. I felt my own timelessness. I had seen him, and I was forever connected to him on the beam of light.

She had a bone-marrow transplant and did well. After the event with the butterflies, her beauty became apparent to everyone around her. She almost radiated pure light. Her simple presence had become a gift to her friends. She had seen her spirit, and it had healed her on a level that was deeper than medicine.

A year later, she is in remission.

Every physician, nurse, and healer knows there is a moment when the spirit begins to heal. Each of us has felt our spirit come back to us when we have felt ill and almost given up. Just when we were out of energy, depressed, and confused, we awakened, and all life looked new. Most of us have heard a doctor say, "I have done all I could do; now it is in the hands of God. If only this patient would get back the will to live."

We believe that the spirit gives us back the will to live, which helps us heal. The spirit is the awakening of the spark that returns a person from death to life. This book is about illuminating the spirit, about finding the light within us that makes us want to wake up in the morning with expectation and delight. It is about finding out who we are and what we are to do that expresses our deepest being.

Use Spirit Body Healing to Help You Change Your Life

We have written *Spirit Body Healing* as a prescriptive book. It tells you what you can do to create immediate change in your life. It tells how to use the Spirit Body Healing method with illnesses—including such life-threatening problems as cancer, AIDS, and heart disease. We have also used the techniques in Spirit Body Healing with people with depression, with trauma, with problems in relationships, and with life crises. The method helps people reconnect with the core of what they believe, with their spirituality. Just as it has helped others, it can help you become a more complete person and have the strength to carry on when things become difficult.

Spirit-Body Healing will also help you "do right action in the world" by getting in touch with the spirit within you, which is connected to the universal spirit. You cannot go outward and see the universe, but you can go inward to the universe within—where your spirit lives—and see the universal spirit.

Spirit Body Healing is not about becoming spiritual or religious in a prescribed conventional sense. You can use *Spirit Body Healing* and have your own personal religious beliefs or even not believe in God. You can deepen the spiritual dimension of your life because the creative person within you is your spiritual teacher.

It might take years of meditation for you to get to this place of spiritual healing. *Spirit Body Healing* is about a more immediate experience of transcendence. In *Spirit Body Healing*, we show you how to reach this place in a moment. How can you take these moments of illumination of the spirit—these flashes—and take them to heal your life?

Use This Book to Heal

We placed each theme gleaned from the Spirit Body Healing research study in its own chapter. Each chapter is arranged in three sections. The first section is the teaching—it tells the stories and explains the theme. The second provides reflections on the theme, to help you use what we as researchers learned. The third section has guided imagery to help you actually feel and experience the themes more deeply. Finally, the prescription at the end of the book has activities and affirmations you can use to heal yourself. The prescription tells you how to follow the pathways into the stories. It invites you to connect with the people's stories, see through their eyes, and benefit from their experience.

Listen, learn, and follow their journeys as your own.

About the Stories

Spirit Body Healing is about exploring the spiritual dimension of your life, about mapping the human heart. The stories taken from our research on healing are a crucial part of the book. The stories of illness or crisis take you to places of spirit that you will remember or recognize. Let the stories take you to a place deep inside yourself, which you have glimpsed but may not yet have grasped. The stories will move you through the places of darkness to the places of light. Do not avoid the places of darkness. They are essential in the process of healing. The stories illuminate the wisdom and beauty found in the darkest of moments.

As we explored the stories, we began to have a sense that inside each story was a moment when you could glimpse the presence of the spirit. We call that moment "an illumination of the spirit." This does not mean there is necessarily an actual light. We use light as a metaphor. In watching the sunrise, there is a moment before the sun rises, when there is just a glimmer. The glimmer is like a membrane between the night and the day. Is there really a membrane between the two? No, but there is a moment, a flash of transition. Before the sun rises, you can see something inside the shadow, which is the coming of the light. The illumination of the spirit is like that glimmer before the sun rises.

About the Reflections

In *Spirit Body Healing* we use reflections as teaching tools, instead of advice or instructions. As you look into the stories of people's lives, it is like looking into a pool of water. As you read the stories, you see a reflection of yourself. You see your own life by seeing other people's lives. As you see into stories of other people's lives, you see through their eyes. As you listen to the wonderful intimacy of their stories, you feel the story in your own body and learn how it is reflected in your own life. Then you can deal with your own story.

The stories are the wooded paths of people who have treaded there before. Follow their paths to a place of illumination, enchantment, and transcendence. Follow those paths to mystical places within their lives. They journeyed far to get there. By following their paths, you hear the echoes of their spirit and glimpse the reflection of your own. The reflections take the points of the story and highlight them and turn them into steps you can use to make the experience happen to you.

About the Guided Imagery

Guided imagery is one of the oldest and most powerful body-mind tools. It comes from all religions and has been used for cancer and heart disease at medical centers all over the world. We use it for Spirit Body Healing. Each chapter includes guided-imagery exercises related to the theme of the chapter. In the imagery, you will feel, hear, see, smell, and taste the experience of spirit for yourself. The guided imagery is a way for you to experience Spirit Body Healing, to embody it, to be there. It is a way to use your own mind's eye to experience Spirit Body Healing.

You Know the Ending Before You Start, So Start the Process with Faith

In the stories, truths are communicated to you through the experiences from people's lives. The difference between your experience as a reader and the participants' experiences is that you will know the ending of the story before you begin. As you read this book, you will know that pain and darkness leads to healing and transcendence. The participants knew only that they were in pain and then went on from there. You will know from the beginning that you are embraced by love and in the presence of your own spirit.

Use Guided Imagery

USING YOUR MIND'S EYE
TO SEE YOUR SPIRIT ILLUMINATED

Guided imagery allows you to experience Spirit Body Healing. With a guided-imagery exercise, in your imagination or mind's eye, you can go into the forest and a butterfly swarm, see the light, and allow the face to appear to you. This guided imagery, like all those in this book, comes from the story. These are the steps people took.

For all guided-imagery exercises, make yourself comfortable. You can be sitting down or lying down. Loosen any tight clothing, uncross your legs and arms. Close your eyes. Let your breathing slow down. Take several deep breaths. Let your abdomen rise as you breathe in and fall as you let your deep breath out. As you breathe in and out, you will become more and more relaxed. You may feel tingling, buzzing, or relaxation. If you do, let those feelings increase. You may feel heaviness or lightness, you may feel your boundaries loosening and your edges softening.

Now let yourself relax. Let your feet relax, let your legs relax. Let the feelings of relaxation spread upward to your thighs and pelvis. Let your pelvis open and relax. Now let your abdomen relax, let your belly expand; do not hold it in anymore. Now let your chest relax, let your heartbeat and breathing take place by themselves. Let your arms relax, your hands relax. Now let your neck relax, your head, your face. Let your eyes relax and see a horizon and blackness for a moment. Let these feelings of relaxation spread throughout your body, let your relaxation deepen. If you wish, you can count your breaths and let your relaxation deepen with each breath.

Now, in your mind's eye, picture yourself in a forest. In your imagination, look around you. It is dawn, the first soft light, the sun is about to rise. The day is warm, you can feel the gentle morning breeze on your face. You can smell the trees, the earth, the air. In front of you is a path that is soft and cleared of underbrush. You can feel the forest floor under your feet as you start walking. You can feel tall grass against the sides of your legs. As you walk, in your mind's eye, look around you. See the sun coming up. As it rises, see the long beams of light coming toward you across the dark forest. See the beams of light coming down from behind the trees, see the air dancing in the light beams, the moisture rising from the forest floor into the bright white columns of light. Let the light beam and the beauty of the forest take you elsewhere. The beams look like they are coming from heaven, like a light from God.

Now, in your mind's eye, see hundreds of butterflies swarming. See the swarm come toward you and stop in the place where the sunbeams came down to Earth in a narrow area. See the perfect circle that the light beams make on the forest floor; see the leaves illuminated, their edges glowing in the morning sun. See how the circle of light looks like a halo. Now the butterfly swarm stops moving; it forms a shape like a face. Let your eyes cross slightly and feel the world open, becoming soft and expansive, deep and hollow. Feel yourself going deeper; feel yourself in a deeper, more expansive place. Look at the face that appears before you. Do you know who it is? Is it God, the Blessed Mother, your loved one, an ancestor? See how the face is glimmering, see the halo of light around it. It is a beautiful sight; let yourself take it in and go even deeper into the vision. Feel how time stands still; feel how the face seemed always to be there. Feel how you have almost seemed always to be there, too. As you look at the face, you can see it speaking to you, you can hear its voice. Listen to the words that the figure in the vision tells you.

Now you see the figure lift its arms as if it were blessing you. In your mind's eye, see a beam of light come out of its hands and come to you. Feel the beam of light come into your heart, and if you want to, pray to the figure you see. Pray or speak to it on the beam of light, tell it what you want, tell it what you want to happen with your life. Feel the love in your heart overflow to the whole universe.

Now, thank him or her for coming to you. Realize that you are as beautiful as anyone throughout time who had ever seen a spiritual vision. Feel your own beauty. Rest there as long as you wish. This is a healing place, a place of spirit, a sacred space. Let yourself return to your room. Move your feet and hands, open your eyes and look around you. Feel your body; it is tingling, full of energy.

When you are ready, return to the room where you are doing the exercise. First move your feet and then move your hands. Move them around and experience the feeling of the movement. Press your feet down onto the floor, feel the grounding, feel the pressure on the bottom of your feet, feel the solidity of the Earth. Feel your backside on the chair; feel your weight pressing downward. Now open your eyes. Look around you. Stand up and stretch, move your body, feel it move. You are back, you can carry the experience of the exercise outward to your life. You will feel stronger and be able to see more deeply. You will be in a healing state. Each time you do the exercise, you will be more relaxed and be able to go deeper and be more deeply healed.

You have seen your spirit, and it has healed you on a level that is deep and full. Your beauty and courage are now visible to everyone who knows you. You can go out into the world with love and positivity and help all those you meet. You have seen your spirit illuminated.

USING YOUR MIND'S EYE
TO SEE YOUR UNIVERSAL SPIRIT

Imagine you are in a spaceship. See yourself flying deep into the universe. Look out of the window. Around you, you see the stars. You are soaring. Look back and see the Earth, see how beautiful she is. See your own life on the Earth, your house, your city. Now look around the spaceship, and see the infinite void from which anything can emerge. Follow the stars to the deepest place in space. Go to the source from which it all comes. See yourself connected to the source in the center of that void. Now see the place of the universal spirit that is within your own body. The same source that created the universe also created you and is within you. The two sources touch. Realize that you and the universe are one.

USING YOUR MIND'S EYE
TO EXPERIENCE THE LIGHT OF THE ESSENCE OF HEALING

In this exercise, you will use guided imagery to relax and feel your spirit heal. To begin, take a deep breath, let your abdomen rise as you breathe in and fall as you breathe out. Now, starting with your head, let your muscles relax. Let your eyes relax, your jaw relax, your neck relax. Let your muscles lengthen, release all tension. Let your arms be supported, feel your fingers drop, let your arms relax, your chest relax. Let your heartbeat and breathing take care of themselves.

Now feel the chair support your body. Feel held, feel your belly relax. In your imagination, see a balloon expand in your belly as you breathe in and get smaller as you breathe out. Now feel your pelvis relax, let it go. Feel it expand and widen. Feel your body get more and more relaxed as you breathe in and out. Feel your legs relax, your feet relax. You are now deeply relaxed. If you have feelings of tingling or buzzing, heaviness or lightness, let them deepen and relax more deeply.

Then, in your mind's eye, go to a place in the center of your body. It can be your belly, your heart, your spine. In your center is a light. It is flickering, soft like a candle flame. Now in your imagination, see this light glowing brighter and brighter. See the sphere of light expand. Feel this light expand around your fingers, feel it expand down to your toes. Feel this soft, warm, translucent, golden light surround you and embrace you. Now in your imagination, feel the light expanding around your body, see the glowing light growing, see your entire body glowing. See the light move beyond the boundaries of your skin, see it expand around you from one foot to two feet away. Feel the light swirling gently, moving. It has a beauty, an ebb and flow. It is soft, it has a rhythm that pulsates like your heart.

Now imagine that this light becomes transformed into the energy of love. Your body is immersed in the glow of living light, and you are being healed, cleansed, you are being loved. The source of this love is a pulsation from within you. Now imagine that this light, this love, and this energy are you. Now in your mind's eye, expand this light to about four feet around you. Now it is interfaced, merged with the light from others around you. You are interconnected, and your love blends with those around you. The light brightens as it interfaces; it becomes magnified in its intensity and flows out of your body. It is spinning, soft, beautiful. Your love is spinning around your own body and the other. You are in a relationship, it is easy, you are in grace and total peace. All you have to do is breathe.

Take a deep breath and allow the light to soften. See the flame flickering inside your heart. In your center, you are grounded in your body. Feel your body being held up by the chair. See the flickering light burning within you. It is the source of your spirit and your love. When you are ready, see yourself back in the room. See the people sitting next to you. You feel refreshed, calm, and centered; you are deeply healed by your own spirit.

Begin to Heal Now

Seeing your spirit will change your life. What reflects the spirit in your life? Everyday experience as simple as a sunrise.

Open your eyes to see your own spirit illuminated. Any way you externalize your inner vision can make your spirit visible to you. A story, a drawing, a joke, a garden, a love poem, a dance, a song, a building—all help you see that there are moments in your life that are sacred. The moment you see your spirit is the moment your heart opens. When you glimpse your spirit, you gasp and cry, you feel emotion, you know who you are. That is the moment you begin to heal.

Chapter 2

The Process of Spirit Body Healing

A Mother Who Made a Basket to Hold Her Spirit

She had just given birth. Her baby was beautiful, but she cried all the time. What was wrong? Why was she so sad when her baby was so beautiful? She got worse; she cried at night and wept quietly during the day. She told this story of how she healed herself:

> One day, I started to make a basket. I do not know where that idea came to me. I bought reed and soaked it and started weaving it. It smelled good, it smelled like the Earth. I touched it and it felt ancient on my hands. As the basket grew, it became round and could hold things. It held me. I let myself go into the basket and rest there in my imagination. I went far back in time, and an old woman came to me in the basket. She sang to me, "You are a wonderful mother, you make a beautiful basket. Look at your baby; she is beautiful. You take wonderful care of her."
>
> As I opened my eyes, I saw my baby was beautiful and I was taking wonderful care of her. The woman continued

singing, a soft lilting song of ancient beauty: "You are whole, you are a wonderful mother, see how she looks at you, your baby, see how her little fingers touch your face when she nurses." And I felt them for the first time, I felt those little fingers and saw the tiny fingernails and how her fingers moved when she was nursing. And I felt encompassed, covered, taken care of deeply.

My depression disappeared as I made more and more baskets. I love my baby and I still make baskets to relax. I give them to my friends. I have not told anyone this story. I hesitate to tell you about the ancient woman; I know it sounds crazy. I am not the kind of person who thinks of things like this. I was not interested in Native American things and certainly not in basketry. But making baskets and hearing the ancient woman is what healed me from my postpartum depression.

The Eight Spirals of Spirit Body Healing

After three years of studying the stories from Mary's research, we found that Spirit Body Healing is an elegant process that takes place like a spiral. For us, the process has eight steps. The experience expands and contracts, expands and contracts. The themes in the stories spin, they appear and turn and are happening at once, within each other, on top of each other. The experience is not linear; rather, it is episodic. One participant said, "For me, healing is like a spiral maze. I walk into the center, thinking I am finished and then I find myself out on the furthest reaches of the spiral again. I draw spirals on my healing pottery to remind me of the nonlinear progress of spirit healing as a process in my life."

1. Pain and darkness

We found that most people start with an experience of pain. They articulate loneliness, grief, fear, psychological pain, physical pain, the pain of a newly diagnosed cancer. From the place of pain, they fall or move into darkness. Darkness is the three-dimensional place where pain lives. It is pain and the person's perception of fear and death.

2. Going elsewhere

Inside the lived experience of darkness, the next themes emerge: going elsewhere, a pause, the trigger, the trigger event. In this step, the person begins to leave pain behind and moves toward healing.

3. The turning point

Next, the participants become immersed in the creative process. They become involved in doing something in their lives: making a garden, going on a trip, making art—painting, sculpting, dancing, journal writing, composing poetry. Becoming creative is a large spiral; how each person becomes involved in creativity differs for each one. Some are invited by friends, some were artists already, some become creative almost by accident.

4. Slipping through the veil

Now the spiral contracts. The participants slip through the veil, they go through a doorway. The witness in themselves appears. This part of the process is about going deeper. Something appears, which they have never seen before.

5. Embodiment of the spirit

The next spiral is the embodiment of Spirit Body Healing. The stories illuminate this experience of attention, breath, and merging with pure spirit.

6. Knowing the truth and trusting the process

This part deals with other themes that emerge: themes of restorying and of transformation. The healing now has an entrancing flow and movement. The person begins to know who she or he is and what he or she needs to do to heal.

7. Healing energy and compassion
When people become creative, they experience deep feelings of compassion for themselves and others.

8. Transcendence
Then they move into the final spiral, a spiral of transcendence that deals with oneness, interconnectedness, luminosity, with seeing God and the angels. This spiral is about receiving love and seeing their whole past as being loved. It is about visionary work and global healing. It is about changing people's whole lives so they are deeply in service to their community. They become different, powerful, and more fully themselves. They heal themselves, others, and the Earth. They are full of energy, intensely alive, and almost messianic about how their creative spirit healed them and how they now want to do projects to help others heal with spirit.

Restory Your Life

After the experience of the eight spirals, they may restory their own lives. They accept the visions, stay with them, and then rewrite their life stories to include the spiritual experience. For example, the woman who saw the face of God in the swarm of butterflies now tells the story of seeing God's face. She thinks of herself in light of that story. The story of her life now includes her remarkable spiritual experience, and she can honor it, receive it, and make it part of her worldview and her self-concept. In her peaceful moments, she holds the vision; in her dark moments, she reaches for it to comfort her.

Many people were not conscious of what created their own healing. It is not necessary for the person to have noted the moment of spirit or to have realized what it was. All that seemed to be necessary was that it was happening. Often, they told us the story and did not even point out that moment or tell us it was special. It had become ordinary, part of their rich lives. As researchers, we listened and tried to figure out what was the healing trigger.

Invite a Peak Spiritual Experience to Come to You

Common to all stories was a moment of spiritual union when the spiritual experience was felt. There was a body and soul communion. Each person had an altered-state experience, an experience where time and space changed, where they were seeing the world in a new way.

Spirit Body Healing invites you to have a peak spiritual experience. We help you get to the place where you can receive it, see it, and remember it. We help you become open and accept it when it comes, claim it as your own without fear, and make it part of your own story.

CHAPTER 3

How Spirit Body Healing Works: Unlocking the Medicine Within

Spirit Body Healing produces a spirit-mind-body shift that changes the blood flow, hormonal balance, and neurotransmitter level in every cell in the body. When the spirit is illuminated, it affects the mind with attitude changes and the body with immune-system optimization. Research on how the spirit heals has traditionally focused on how thoughts, emotions, and images change blood flow and hormone balance in the body. This research in mind-body medicine has contributed much to our understanding of how a person's attitude and worldview effects healing. The research has contributed to the incorporation of techniques such as meditation, relaxation, guided imagery, and support into mainstream medical care when treating conditions such as cancer and AIDS.

Contemporary research on prayer has broadened our understanding of mind-body medicine to include what has been called spirit or soul. This chapter explains the research in mind-body medicine and the research in prayer, to give the reader a brief overview on how spirit heals. Researchers have found that art and prayer have the same physiological effects on the body, and both lead to healing.

The Spiritual Experience Is Perceived as Imagery

As people experience Spirit Body Healing, they experience events perceived as images. The woman who saw the face of God in the butterfly swarm saw an image. The images can involve any one of the five senses or all of them at once. The person perceives the event as a thought, an emotion, or a sensory experience of a voice or vision or both. The event need not be clear or like a movie in intensity. It can simply be like a creative idea. It can be visual, auditory, tactile, olfactory, or gustatory.

Images of peak spiritual experiences are first held in areas that are responsible for thought and for instituting muscle movement. The discharges of neurons come from both the memory of the vision and the implementation of the process that makes the image more real, such as making art.

The people having the experience feel that a thought, an idea, or an image of a spiritual experience comes from outside of them or from their mind. For many people, it feels as though it comes from the imagination or memory. Others feel it comes from God or from spirit. Because spiritual experiences are so ancient and involve so many proprioceptive sensory and motor pathways, the experiences appear very real and intense as a person gets in touch with them.

Our Bodies Have Evolved to Be Healed with Spiritual Visions

We believe that many of these memories of images or movements are ancient and have been flickering steadfastly within the human brain as it evolved. When these visions come to the surface of our consciousness and are released, we experience deep healing. Humans have had visions of spirits and gods from the earliest recorded history. Healings have accompanied these visions. The visions change physiology to produce the healing state.

When you translate images in your mind into an activity such as making art or making a garden, the images make muscle movements that produce a deep level of concentration. The process takes your whole attention and takes you away from worries and concerns of the outer world. This happens automatically. You do not need to do anything except to focus intensely. The ancient neural pathways of the mind take over, and you are taken elsewhere, to a mental state of pure concentration that most resembles meditation.

The physiology that results from this state is similar to the physiology of prayer and meditation, involving deep relaxation and healing. Herbert Benson, of the Behavioral Medicine Clinic at Harvard University Medical School, wrote about this in his classic *The Relaxation Response*. He showed that meditation alone lowered blood pressure, heart rate, and breathing rate, and that it was a primary therapy for heart-disease patients. Today, Dean Ornish uses meditation as a major part of his heart-disease regimen, to reduce stress. He also uses it for its spiritual focus, to reduce alienation and promote feelings of connectedness and oneness.

The Three Ways Spiritual Experiences Change Every Cell in Your Body

The images of spiritual experience result in the firing of neurons in different areas of the brain. The neurons connect to the rest of the body in three simple ways.

1. Spirit changes your nervous system

Images held in the right brain activate the hypothalamus. The hypothalamus activates the autonomic nervous system and results in arousal or relaxation through a two-part balancing system that affects the whole body, touching virtually every cell. The autonomic nervous system is a healing system that balances and maintains the blood flow, heartbeat, breathing rate, and hormone level needed for any activity we are doing. This system was thought to work by itself, but it is now known to be profoundly influenced by thoughts.

The autonomic nervous system has two branches: the sympathetic and the parasympathetic. The sympathetic branch of the autonomic nervous system is the branch that controls "fight or flight," creating the physiology necessary to run from a perceived threat, such as a tiger, or to assume a defensive posture. When the large hemispheres of the brain hold the neurological pattern of an image of a threat, they alert the hypothalamus, causing sympathetic arousal and speeding up the heartbeat, increasing breathing, sending blood to the large muscles, flooding the body with adrenaline and stress hormones, and creating a physiology of alertness. The memory of running away from a threat, such as escaping from a tiger, or of facing it and fighting and getting away takes us through a whole cycle of experience. When you are out of danger at last, the feeling of safety relieves tension and puts you in a state of release. The cycle is called the arousal/release cycle, and it charts each person's way of reacting to any exciting event.

On the other hand, the stimulation of the parasympathetic branch of the autonomic nervous system results in relaxation, healing, body repair, and preventive maintenance. When the brain perceives an image of a peaceful scene, of a spiritual vision, of making art, of creativity, of prayer, it alerts the hypothalamus to trigger parasympathetic arousal, and the heartbeat slows, blood pressure drops, breathing slows, blood goes to the intestines, and the whole body changes. The vision or dance movement of a soft caress stimulates the circuits that remember deep relaxation, creating that physiology. We now have the physiology of healing, of creativity, of prayer.

2. Spirit changes your hormonal system

This model gives us an idea of how your mind is connected to your body and how images and muscle movements stimulate your entire being. When you have a peak spiritual experience, the area of the cerebrum that holds images of muscle movement is stimulated, sending messages to the hypothalamus that allow you to respond to the imagery. If the image is one of deep joy or release of tension, your body is put in a healing state through the hypothalamic pathways of the parasympathetic nervous system. When you experience pain and you see that vision for the first time, you feel yourself release the tension around the pain. Relaxation ensues, and the healing physiology is started.

The experience of spirit also affects the body through the hormonal system. As the nerve cells discharge like a loom of light flashing through your brain, the hypothalamus also sends messages to the adrenal glands to release epinephrine (adrenaline) and other hormones, which travel throughout your body and are picked up by receptors that cause some cells to contract, others to relax, some to act, others to rest. Your entire physiology is changed a second time by a spirit experience, an image or movement held in your brain. The second change is chemical, resulting from hormonal shifts. It is slower, but it is just as profound, in that it affects almost every cell in the body. So when you see God or the Blessed Mother, this experience changes the hormonal flow to each cell in your whole body. That changes your blood pressure, pulse, respiratory rate, and the blood flow to your heart and brain.

3. Spiritneuroimmunology: Spirit changes your immune system

The third way in which experiences of spirit affect the body is in the realm of the neurotransmitter. Here, the spiritual experience causes specific areas of the brain to release endorphins and other neurotransmitters that affect brain cells and the cells of the immune system. The neurotransmitters relieve pain and make the immune system function more efficiently. They cause killer T cells to eat cancer cells, white blood cells to attack viruses, and generally change the body's ability to respond to illness. So when you have an experience of spirit, when you make art or music, or dance, or picture an image that is freeing and joyful, your body actually changes its physiology to heal itself.

The release of the endorphins when we experience a vision of spirit is deeply pleasurable. It is like exercising: Endorphins are like opiates or other mind-altering drugs, and they make us feel expanded, connected, at one, relaxed, vibrating, tingling, at peace. The endorphins function like mind-altering chemicals to produce and enhance the spiritual experience and make it more real. In a real sense, the release of endorphins during prayer and spiritual visions may be the major healing force. *Psychoneuroimmunology* is a term that puts together *psycho* for the mind, *neuro* for the nerve nets of the brain, and *immune* for the immune system, to describe how thoughts or images in the mind affect the immune system. In this book, we call it *spiritneuroimmunology* because spirit causes the immune system to work at its optimum and eat cancer cells, viruses, and other unwelcome invaders.

Longevity and the Spirit

Studies in parallel fields have results applicable to Spirit Body Healing. Two studies have shed particular light on how spirit heals: David Spiegel's study at Stanford, showing that women with metastatic breast cancer lived twice as long when they were in support groups, as compared with women without support, and Fawzy's study from UCLA, showing that people with melanoma lived longer and had fewer recurrences when they were given ten hours of structured support and education, as compared with those having no support or education. These two dramatic studies of life extension with relatively minimal mind-body interventions led us to postulate that an involved intervention such as a person having a peak spiritual experience, could be very beneficial.

Spirit Body Healing uses the core concepts of support, the release of fear, attitude change, and feeling connected. Spirit Body Healing and support groups, in fact, have much in common. The visions of spirit that people see are visions of caring, of loving, of honoring themselves. Spiritual experiences have given people deep support. Knowing you are loved by Jesus is the greatest possible support for a person who is a religious Christian. Spiritual visions have also provided meaning and coherence to a person. Carl Jung said that his patients who believed in God and in an afterlife did better with life-threatening illness than did those who were atheists and had no belief in an afterlife. He said that whether or not God existed and an afterlife or reincarnation were proven, the belief clearly proved beneficial to people in their healing.

Prayer and Relationships Heal

Extensive research on prayer and healing helps us understand the importance of Spirit Body Healing. In one study, people prayed for patients who had had a heart attack and were in an intensive-care unit. Patients who were prayed for did better than those who were not, even if they did not know they were being prayed for. Plants grow faster when they are being prayed for. Prayer has been demonstrated to help people heal.

Dean Ornish has shown that people do better in all illnesses when they have relationships. People do worse when their loved one dies or they are alienated and alone. Spiritual experiences make people feel connected and help with feelings of alienation. They also help people deal with grief. Support from church groups and from someone to speak to each day help people in a way similar to help from a support group.

Healing Energy Involves Nerves and Blood Vessels Producing Healing

Perhaps less scientific, but more universal in experience is healing energy. Healing with the spirit releases the life force, a force from the collective consciousness. The spirit infuses us with the creative process that is alive and on fire. In healing, force, energy, and consciousness are the same. In the Hindu religion, energy and matter are related to consciousness. Inside matter and energy is consciousness. When you heal with the spirit, you go inside to the place of consciousness and slip through the membrane into the place of the spirit.

When you experience healing, you feel energy. You feel this freeing of energy as a buzzing, a tingling, a vibration. You feel the energy as a sensation that can flow throughout the body, from body to body, from the universe to us. It can be seen by psychics and meditators, and it is often portrayed in visionary art. This energy has been called chi, prana, kundalini, God's breath, acupuncture energy meridians, chakras, and the life force; it has been described throughout all time and is an integral part of the human experience.

When the spirit is illuminated, energy is involved. Perhaps the simplest metaphor for Spirit Body Healing is that it frees our body's healing energy to flow. The spirit soars, goes home, and unites with the deep source; energy is released like a waterfall.

Part Two

The Eight Steps of Spirit Body Healing

Chapter 4

Step One: Go into Your Own Pain and Darkness

The Woman with the Golden Dove of Love

The first thing she told us was that she had breast cancer with more than ten lymph nodes positive for cancer. Her doctor told her that this type of breast cancer can be fast growing and can spread and that it was "something to worry about." As she said this, she looked down and almost seemed as though she would start crying right in the middle of her first sentence. She was forty-five years old, and her husband had just left her, in a bitter divorce. She felt lonely, abandoned, betrayed, terrified of dying, and extremely depressed. Things in her life had gone from bad to worse and were not getting better. She told us the story of her husband leaving her for a younger woman, his taking her house, her crying every night. But mostly she talked about death. She said she expected to die, and each day she awakened, that was all she could think about. Then, after that thought, she would hate.

She would think about how much she hated her husband for what he had done, and she was especially angry at him for taking their summer house from her. He knew this was the only place on Earth she loved, and now it, too, was gone from her. It was a symbol of losing all she had. It was all being taken from her, and there was nothing she could do.

As she told her story, she looked terrible. She was hunched over and looked like an old woman. Yet we looked at her and saw how beautiful she was. We could see what she had looked like when she was young. We could see both her beauty and her power. As she told her dark stories, we looked at her, and we both thought she could tell that she was being seen as a beautiful woman. She started to look a little better, to speak more clearly, to cry less. We asked her what was the most beautiful experience she had ever had. She closed her eyes and said:

> That is easy. I know the most wonderful experience I have ever had. I was in a meditation retreat. I had been sitting for three days. Things were not going well. I was depressed and felt unsuccessful. Even in my meditation I could not get out of my feelings of worthlessness and pain. It seemed to me like my whole life was under water, that I was drowning, that there was nothing I could do.
>
> And then it happened. Right in my meditation, a hole appeared in my chest. It was not an ordinary hole; it was an opening. A place of fire. It had edges of flames around it, its center was light. It was a light like I have never seen before. It shimmered and wavered and opened further for me. So I went in. I knew my body was still sitting in meditation and I was going into my image at once. I saw a dove sitting in my chest. It was golden, and it sat in a circle of blue. It spoke to me. Not in words, rather I felt its meaning in my whole existence. It filled me with its golden light. It opened my heart. I realized that it lived next to my heart. I realized it was always there. And most importantly I realized that it loved me. I went into that dove and was the dove and was surrounded by it, too. I was full of energy, and I was larger and

more powerful. It was me and it was inside me and more than me.

I had never had such an experience. I was taken back. I had never in my life, and never have since, felt that wonderful. I felt like I was at home. I felt like I belonged right where I was. I felt deeply as if I had been loved forever. I knew that I was part of something much larger than my concerns. I was in the presence of God.

As she told us this story, she sat upright, and her beauty emerged. We could see that she was becoming who she used to be and wanted to be again. The vision occurred during a retreat, and she had forgotten it and never used its power. In her illness, it was gone and not accessible to her. Now, seeing the vision from her past had helped her regain her power and strength, and it was hers forever. She could go there whenever she wanted to; she could be in the presence of her dove whenever she became afraid or depressed.

We saw her a year later. She looked radiant. She told us she was in a relationship, she was in love. She told us that she felt so alive, so full of light, so different from when we had seen her a year before. She said, "It is as if my own spirit as that dove came out of me and took me and healed me. My own spirit awakened and told me she loved me and made my body sit up and feel again."

Pain is the Doorway to Spirit Body Healing

Anyone who is ill feels pain. Whether it is the fear of death that haunts cancer patients or the chronic pain that wears down arthritis patients or the sadness and desperation that makes people with severe depression suicidal, pain and suffering are hallmarks of being ill. So it is not surprising that the overall experience of Spirit Body Healing begins in a place of pain. Pain is the first theme to emerge from the stories, which vividly describe the characteristics of pain. One man who told us his story is suffocating and can't breathe, and he finds out that he has Hodgkin's lymphoma; one woman screams with pain in fibromyalgia; another woman feels she cannot go on one more moment after her divorce. For all the participants in our study, pain is a compelling return to dark memories. It is the experience that provides the doorway to Spirit Body Healing.

A Bowl Took Away My Pain

Spirit Body Healing helps people deal with both physical and psychological pain. Gina, a minister and teacher, vividly discussed her experience of being in physical pain and finding her spirit:

> I was in my mid-twenties, and I developed pelvic inflammatory disease from a Dalkon shield birth-control device. I was in a little hospital in Maine in a horrible little green room, and I was scared out of my mind. I hurt more than I could imagine. My belly was hot like it was on fire. Waves of pain went through me like knives; it was like I was being tortured. Then I had a drug reaction that almost killed me. I had trouble breathing, and I got a skin rash that itched and made me look swollen. Now I was in pain and could not breathe, and my skin was too sensitive to touch. Looking back on it all, I think I was a lot closer to death than I realized. I felt sick beyond belief.
>
> Then from within the darkness and the pain, a dear friend brought me a large, beautiful, brightly colored Italian bowl for my twenty-fifth birthday. It became my only visual reference in the whole room, and so it became my focal point. When the pain worsened and I became more frightened, I would find myself staring into this bowl. It was my first ex-

perience of a mandala [a circular form filled with images, which has been used for thousands of years in many cultures to facilitate concentration and meditation]. It became a really important discovery for me.

Then I got an idea. I do not know where it came from. I had a close friend bring in my camera, and I began to photograph the bowl and then the other objects on the bedside table. I would photograph the shelves and the flowers and any object that was compelling to me. Suddenly, I realized that when I was looking through the camera, I was not afraid and I was not in pain. I would go into the experience of seeing the beauty of each object and lose myself in it for a small period of time. When I could concentrate on beauty, I did not feel the pain and could begin to heal.

Move from Pain to Beauty

Gina described beginning her journey into healing as moving from a place of pain and fear to a place of concentration and beauty. Her description of being in a pain that had her whole attention and feeling as if she was facing death is common to many participants in this study. Gina discovered the mandala as a way to focus and to go into a place of beauty. In that moment, she forgot the fear and became involved in her creative process. She said that her illness itself became her doorway into the spiritual world. She spoke of a sense of focusing on something outside herself. She discovered an opportunity to become one with spirit. Gina now teaches hospital chaplains to use spirit and art to heal.

My Shamanic Transformation

Christiane is a brilliant, eccentric artist. The mother of two young girls, she was in a difficult point in her life, confused about her marriage and about who she was. She was extremely depressed and suicidal. She told us her story of going into her psychological pain.

In this story, Christiane mentions many of the factors that other participants share about going inward to pain. She feels her own death. She describes it as the bottom of the world. She describes all her connections breaking. She loses herself inside her pain. She has a dream or a memory. Finally, she turns to do something with some creative process. This experience of suffering in pain is the beginning. Pain triggers a return to the self. Christiane tells her story:

> I was constantly miscarrying, and during those periods of time, I had to be very still. I'm a very active person, and my body has to move every day or I'm not really happy, so that was horribly difficult. I would be on the couch, and I think what happened was that I would go into trances. I did that on almost a daily basis, just to get through this. Sometimes I would see wonderful things and experience things internally that were extremely satisfying and beautiful.
>
> At the time, I came across a book by Joan Halifax, called *Shamanic Voices*. I started to read the book, and it was as though the things I was seeing took the shape of the people's experiences. These were shamans, and they were all describing pain and how their initiation had occurred and the visions they had had. What was so amazing to me was that I would see something that was completely culturally separate from my understanding of what it should look like. I started wondering if I would see their visions. That just seemed wild and wonderful.
>
> But then we were able to have children, and I put that all aside and didn't use it until after our second daughter was born. This was a period of about six years between these two times in my life. When that happened, I expected everything to be hunky-dory, but I went into a place of great darkness—a place of tremendous psychic pain that I

couldn't get out of. I felt as though I was going to die, I really did. I just couldn't believe that you could live with that much pain and stay alive. Everything was falling apart around me. Everything I believed in, everything that had been helpful to me, that had been connected to me, just went away, and I found myself in a spot that felt like the bottom of the world, and in order to find myself again, I turned to visions, shamanism, and creativity.

Use Books As Tools to Start Your Journey

Many participants told stories of using books in their healing. One woman used Jean Shinoda Bolen's *Pilgrimages* and had her first experience of ritual after she read it. Books and spiritual work often precede by months or even years the experience of healing. Many of the participants had experiences of going on meditation retreats, going to classes where spiritual techniques were taught, or going to women's groups.

It is as if the patients had been preparing all their lives. Resources they did not know they had came into play. From the darkness and pain come the tools, the learnings, the meditation techniques that emerge and help the person find the spirit to heal.

Christiane talked about her personal experience of shamanism. Other participants also have shamanic experiences. The shamans go into their personal place of pain and darkness and come out with visions that heal them and make them healers. This story of going from darkness to visions is common in many world cultures, from Siberian tribes to Buddhist monasteries.

The Caregiver's Pain

A pediatric oncologist leans over the hospital bed of a dying child. It is late at night after a long day's work. After twenty-five years of caring for dying children, his spirit weeps. It has been a long, hard road. He feels as if his work has taken its toll on him. He leaves the child to go from the hospital and get in his car to drive away. He leaves behind the mother and her grief. He walks down the long, empty corridors on the way to the parking lot. He pauses and takes out a pencil. He writes a poem about the child he was taking care of.

Going into this space of spirit calms him. It helps him see the child as beautiful. He reaches deep inside himself for words that resonate with his own experience, words that connect him deeply to the dying. Does the poem bring the physical into a new way of seeing and relating that is the voice of his spirit? The physician-poet sees beauty and merges with the patient. His care is changed, and his way of being as a healer is changed forever. He writes in a small notebook. In the middle of his hard, busy day, he jots down first lines of poems in the hall. He says that the poems help him deal with the pain of his own grief. They keep him alive and help him keep practicing medicine. He sees beauty in very dark situations and can handle it much better because of his poetry. Seeing his spirit helps him deal with the physical pain of his patients and his own psychological pain. Spirit helps him grieve for the children.

Transforming Fear into Serenity

After people experience pain, they often face fear. Gina tells this story of dealing with fear:

> I felt anger and despair. My fear was huge. It was like a dark beast that was so enormous, and it had me by the throat. I couldn't see anything but the darkness. I remember sitting in a chapel and the fear was so enormous that I was in terror of letting it in. My heart was pounding. I was hyperventilating, and I decided I had to face the fear.

So I gave the fear permission to enter the room with me and I could hear it coming down the hallway. I heard it first. Then I could feel its breathing. My heartbeat was escalating. It was enormous—it was black, it was scary, and it was huge, and it was terrifying, but as soon as I started looking at it, it began to diminish and it began to speak to me. It told me that it had been my protector and that it had really sought to defend me from something my system thought was going to kill me. It told me it was afraid I wasn't going to need it anymore. Now I knew I really didn't, but it had become such a huge part of me that I couldn't release it.

Then, this amazing thing happened. I took pity on it, and it began to shrink, and it got smaller and smaller until it was maybe the size of a horse. It lay down in the center of the chapel, and I went up, held its head in my lap, and stroked it. I realized how we had served each other and how thankful I had to be for it. I realized how much compassion I had for its suffering because basically it had taken on my illness.

I portrayed the fear as a series of sculptural pieces. They were very confrontational for me, terrifying to work on, but extraordinarily healing. It was a big risk for me because I was making them in a public studio where I was teaching, and they were very dark, and in the piece, they translated into a character I called the "Tiger Woman." I met a lot of physical resistance when I began the pieces, and then I fell in love with them and I found compassion for the pieces, which became one ensemble piece. It contained a baby on its back.

Other people who were in really deep emotional distress asked if they could borrow the piece and used it and lived with it and used it in their own healing. I could stop fighting the fear, and because I could see it, it didn't have this enormous power over me. When I had it as a physical object, a piece of sculpture, then I could work with it. I went into a place of serenity and, you know, the heart palpitations relaxed and I could look at the darkness and it was not so frightening.

Turn Fear into Compassion

Gina's narrative reveals a thematic way of understanding fear. Her story suggests fear as something that approaches her. Her way of dealing with this fear is to make art. In the art, she becomes the *Tiger Woman*. The tiger woman will protect the baby at all costs. In making *Tiger Woman*, she reclaims a lost dimension. She restories the illness and reclaims her baby. Is this baby she has made the baby she has lost from becoming infertile during her pelvic inflammatory disease illness? In the making of her art, she tells her own story. She vows to risk her own life to preserve the life of this baby. The meaning of her art involves the relationship of her fear and the consequences of her illness. She is healing her own life as she saves this baby, the baby that emerged from the darkness of this illness.

Pain Deepens to Darkness

The participants in the study began to remember stories of disturbing dreams, memories of childhood, or incidents of pain or fear in the past. The experience of pain was so great, there was the opportunity to glimpse the death of the self. Pain gave the participants a path to see the death of a past way of being, in which they were attached to a certain life.

Then a shift took place; the process deepened. Pain led them to a deeper darkness that involved their whole life. The event became the pathway to the inner world. The divorce, cancer, whatever it was became an event that preceded falling into darkness. Then the darkness took over the person's life. All of the participants told of a sense of being taken by the darkness. There they experienced existential loneliness. They often said, "Everything I once believed is over." The questioning of meaning or a loss of meaning takes over. The diagnosis of cancer turned into a veil that covered their whole lives and blocked the light of the simplest day. It was as if they were suddenly looking through a filter that kept them from being ordinary anymore.

Each participant started from a different place of pain, so each person had an individual darkness. One had Hodgkin's lymphoma and was dying, and her darkness was the fear of not having lived and of losing everything. One had breast cancer and was afraid of leaving her children. One had ovarian cancer, was very angry, and had demons to slay. These people were all facing life-threatening illnesses, and they were afraid they were going to die.

Others face pain and not death. One woman with fibromyalgia faced chronic pain and was suffering each moment. She did not feel anyone believed her as she was withering away. Her darkness was an inability to be taken seriously. Another woman was undergoing a difficult divorce. Her darkness was a body racked with pain from emotional anger and abandonment. One woman faced loneliness in a marriage full of alienation. Another woman's whole life was in crisis, and she could not go on with each day.

A physician was dealing with his own alienation. After years of working in the hospital, he began to write poetry. A man with a wife having a bone-marrow transplant used prayer and a journal to deal with grief and to deal with the hospitalization of his wife; he tried to give her what she needed to make it through. A child dying of a brain tumor was frightened and lonely. She knew she would lose her life and would have to say good-bye to her mother. She wondered how she would do this—her mother seemed so scared and could not talk to her about death.

A Dream Emerges from the Darkness

Christiane tells more of her story:

> I was at the very darkest time of this transformation, and I was really at the end of my rope. I can remember driving in my car and yelling at the top of my lungs, "Help, Help! I can't go on any longer." I had been doing that for months and I was exhausted.
>
> Then one night, out of the most profound darkness, I received this dream that was so big. In the dream, I was with my two children. I was holding them because they had no arms. I was dreaming a whole series of dreams of women without arms, especially myself. I had my little child who was three or four in my arms, and the other one I had my arm around. We were walking into a place that was very similar to the Natural History Museum in New York. That is one of my favorite places and where I get a lot of my ideas and inspiration. The people who made all of the ceremonial objects there are my spiritual friends.
>
> We were going up the stairs. I was very concerned about why we were there, and when we got to the top of the stairs, I noticed a woman reclining on a couch. She was wearing a man's military coat from the Second World War. It was very heavy, and I wondered why she was doing that. It was almost as though there was a war going on for her. She looked in huge pain. I went up to her and I said, "What's going on? Why are you in so much pain? Can I help?" And she said, "I have to be who I am." I blinked and looked at her, and her arms and legs were gone. I just gasped, my God, how painful. Then I blinked again and looked again. Now her head was gone.
>
> I said to her, "Is it necessary to go through this much pain in order to be who you are?" I blinked again, and the answer was this incredible transparent woman. She was about thirty-

six inches long, and I remember she had very long black hair. You could see through her, and you could see these sort of flowing areas of color in ribbons. There were different colors just going through her, and you could see everything that was going on inside her completely. She was the most exquisite creature I have ever seen. I was overwhelmed. I was crying and I was in awe. I had never seen anything like this, and I just knew I needed to be this woman. I had to be completely transparent.

The way I translated that into life in a more real way was to make a body casting of myself as the open woman. I made myself a woman that you go right through. So in a way I created her so that I could become her. I felt the transformation was very much about allowing my children to be powerful women in their own right in this world. If I couldn't access my own power, then they would never find theirs, or they would, perhaps, but with tremendous pain and difficulty. Something made me do something real in the outer world to manifest my visions outside me.

Remember Things Past

Crucial in the process of spirit healing is remembrance. When people go into the darkness, they remember. They remember dreams, childhood incidents, moments of great pain, and moments of great brightness. The memories become the subjects of the process of healing. They remember the issues that are central to their lives. They are put in the places where they must solve key problems that have haunted them all along. The spirit becomes illuminated and helps them on the way.

Extract Your Pain

The theme of going into the darkness is also about the extraction of pain. In Mary's own healing process, when she painted her first painting, *Cut Out My Heart*, she was extracting the pain from her chest, taking it out of her body. She says, "I felt severe physical pain. I was hunched over, protecting myself from the real world. When I painted, I moved. I opened my chest. I visualized the pain, I extracted it. To be able to see it, there was a process of extracting it out of me so I could then see it."

For a person in great pain, falling into the darkness and extracting the pain is like a surgical removal. You remove something from you that is dark and is about suffering. It could be sorrow, pain, fear, or death.

Reflections on Pain and Darkness

The first step in Spirit Body Healing is going into the darkness and coming out with the beginning of healing. Know that healing begins only from darkness. Every person who heals must start from darkness. You are not alone. Honor your darkness, respect it. You need not like it or want to be there, but know it is the inevitable first step to healing, growth, and change. Do everything you can to get out of the pain. Don't stay there to heal, but don't avoid facing it, and realize that at the end, it will be the doorway to healing. If you can, face the darkness head on. Do something to externalize it, draw it, write about it, tell the story of it to someone you trust who is loving and accepting.

When you realize the darkness is the place to start, the first thing you can do is look for your dreams or memories that start you going inward. See the visions in the darkness as your beginning of your journey to healing. Next, take the dreams, memories, visions, and focus outside yourself. Or just focus outside yourself on anything that takes your attention. Like Gina with her bowl, you can leave the place of your suffering and go into the beauty around you. Like Christiane with her dreams, you can see your start within the visions that come to you.

Look for a Glimmer in the Darkness

Look for the first light to appear in the darkness. Look around you for any spiritual messages or joyful ideas to come to you. We know this is hard, and it seems almost impossible when you are in the deepest pain. Recall, however, that when Gina saw her bowl and realized it was beautiful, she also had her first glimpse of the spirit behind the beauty. She saw the part of herself that could see beauty, and she realized she, too, was beautiful. Look for the light that surrounds you even in your deepest darkness.

Many of the participants who shared their stories of healing with us also turned to resources they had. They told us of using books, meditation, skills they had learned from their life before they became ill. Everything you have learned is useful to you now. Each thing you did in your life has given you a skill that is crucial to your healing now. If you have learned to use computers, taken classes in cooking, gone to women's groups or moon groups, or taken meditation classes with natural childbirth, use the center of that learning now to let yourself expand and change. Turn to visions and shamanism and creative work of some kind. This journey in Spirit Body Healing will be a journey into your inner world, into the world of visions. Both shamanism and creative work are the best ways of taking the visions and making them real for you.

By *shamanism*, we mean traditional ways of seeing spirit, which include intuition, dreaming, daydreaming, seeing inward, imagery journeys, and making healing art. Shamanism is not unusual or strange; it is the ancient way of seeing spirit that humans have perfected for thousands of years.

Invite the Light

When you bring the fear, pain, and darkness outside yourself so you can see it as a vision or dream, it starts to become your healer. When you write it, draw it, or dance it, it grows and changes from fear and darkness to a healing voice and vision. In this way of looking at things, pain is the opportunity to let go of your old self. It is the shedding of the chrysalis. From within the darkness, a tiny light emerges. Invite this light and wait for the big dream that will change your life. Look around you and find someone to take you there. Find friends, artists, healers, teachers. They will come from the most ordinary people in your life. They will come from unexpected places. Do not judge. Accept lessons and teachings from all around you. Beginner's mind is good. Surprise is good. Realize it is a process that takes time. Have patience, let it happen. This is only the first step to your healing.

Use Guided Imagery

USING YOUR MIND'S EYE
TO MAKE PAIN YOUR DOORWAY TO HEALING

Make yourself comfortable. You can be sitting down or lying down. Loosen tight clothing, uncross your legs and arms. Close your eyes. Let your breathing slow down. Take several deep breaths. Let your abdomen rise as you breathe in and fall as you let your deep breath out. As you breathe in and out, you will become more and more relaxed. You may feel tingling, buzzing, or relaxation. If you do, let those feelings increase. You may feel heaviness or lightness, you may feel your boundaries loosening and your edges softening.

Now let yourself relax. Let your feet relax, let your legs relax. Let the feelings of relaxation spread upward to your thighs and pelvis. Let your pelvis open and relax. Now let your abdomen relax, let your belly expand; do not hold it in any more. Now let your chest relax, let your heartbeat and breathing take place by themselves. Let your arms relax, your hands relax. Now let your neck relax, your head, your face. Let your eyes relax; see a horizon and blackness for a moment. Let these feelings of relaxation spread throughout your body. Let your relaxation deepen. If you wish, you can count your breaths and let your relaxation deepen with each breath.

Now from within this safe place of relaxation, in your mind's eye, go to a place of pain that is physical. It is a place of pain that is holding a tension, fire, inflammation, illness or swelling. You can go to that place and begin there. Or you can scan your body to find a pressure, an emptiness, a density, a hurt, a physical experience of anxiety. Go to the place where that pain is located, and breathe yourself into that place softly, slowly, and gently. Breathe, and in your mind's eye, go to that place and rest there, and allow yourself to observe whatever images and thoughts come. The lesson is allowing them to be and letting them unfold.

Let an image appear of a painful sensation in your life. If you have an illness, it can be something that has taken place since you became ill, or it can be something from far in your past. It need not be the most painful experience you have had; it can be something that was difficult. From the safe place you are now in, while continuing to breathe deeply, go back to that event. See it as vividly as you can. Feel how your body felt, see what is around you, smell any odors present, hear sounds around you. Remember you are not there now, you are in the room here, what you are letting come to you is a memory. Let the memory surround you, feel what it was like being in that pain.

Release the pain, letting it go forth. Remember that pain is a doorway for you to become stronger. As you experience the pain and darkness, let your strong self emerge. Let it grow within you. Feel the energy in your body increase and help you in the place of pain.

As you feel how your body feels, as you hear sounds and see images, pay attention to any other memories that come to you. If there are older images, dreams, older memories that come to you now, just be with them, allow them to vibrate, and release them. Breathing into them, be there, feel how your body feels, smell the air, see images, hear voices. Let yourself be there fully.

Realize you are healing. You are safe here in the room, protected by your prayers. If you wish, imagine that someone you love and trust goes with you into the darkness and stays with you there, protecting you and keeping you company. This person will help to see that nothing happens to you that you cannot handle. Remember you are not alone. If the darkness is too uncomfortable, come back to the room and open your eyes. Do only what you can handle. You can try the exercise again later. Remember, this pain has already been within you. You can handle it because you have been holding it so long. In the darkness, we have the opportunity to embrace pain with love; in darkness is spiritual love. Cradle your pain in the openness of your own heart.

※

If you have been in psychotherapy, you remember that you told your therapist about your deepest pain for fifty minutes, then you left. You then spent twenty-four hours a day with your experience of pain and darkness. Once you left the office, you were with your pain again yourself. These exercises take you to your pain, like a therapist does. The message of this book, however, is that you are not alone, not forsaken. The angels are with you twenty-four hours a day. That is what the stories tell us, this book re-creates the experience of not being alone. This is very powerful. Once you experience your pain in the guided imagery, you will also experience love.

Night is the time you can see the vastness of our universe. Only at night can you see the infinite. At night you can see past your house and see the stars, past the Earth to the galaxies; you see spaciousness, you see the truth of reality. If you move out of the darkness of the night, into the day, you see the present in your life. Darkness is your opportunity to see past the distortion of light. In the darkness is your best opportunity to see deeper into yourself, into your fear, your pain, and discover you are. If darkness is the three-dimensional place where pain lives, it is the infinite three-dimensional space where you can find that the universe is filled with millions of suns, and your spirit is as large as it all. Spirit Body Healing is about merging with the presence of God, who is as large as the universe; the way you embody the presence of God is to go deep into the infinite darkness and merge with Him.

USING YOUR MIND'S EYE TO MAKE YOURSELF LARGER THAN THE PAIN

Make yourself comfortable. You can be sitting down or lying down. Loosen any tight clothing, uncross your legs and arms. Close your eyes. Let your breathing slow down. Take several deep breaths. Let your abdomen rise as you breathe in and fall as you breathe out. As you breathe in and out, you will become more and more relaxed. You may feel tingling, buzzing, or relaxation. If you do, let those feelings increase. You may feel heaviness or lightness, you may feel your boundaries loosening and your edges softening.

Let yourself relax. Let your feet relax, let your legs relax. Let the feelings of relaxation spread upward to your thighs and pelvis. Let your pelvis open and relax. Now let your abdomen relax, let your belly expand. Let your chest relax, let your heartbeat and breathing take place by themselves. Let your arms relax, your hands relax. Let your neck relax, your head relax, your face relax. Let your eyes relax; see a horizon and blackness for a moment. Let these feelings of relaxation spread through your body, let your relaxation deepen. If you wish, you can count your breaths and let your relaxation deepen with each breath.

Now focus on whatever it is in your life that causes suffering. It can be a physical pain, emotional pain, anxiety, a frantic feeling, depression, or an illness or disease. Focus on it, allow it to exist where it resides, feel it, breathe around it. Allow the feeling or the emotion to be, let it intensify. Breathe life into it like a fire, watch the embers of the pain burn. Allow the unbearable to be there, allow the despair to exist where it does. Don't hold back, allow the experience of pain to be with you completely. Allow it to live within you, recognize your own suffering. Feel it, see it, look into the face of your own pain. Move with it, move into it. It pulsates and has a reason for being; it is alive. Do not ask why, just be with it. Allow it to reveal itself to you in its authenticity. Allow yourself to cry, scream, shake, vibrate; allow the pain to release itself through your body.

Move into the place where the pain holds the greatest intensity and density, where it grows in momentum like a dam that is going to burst. It is astonishing there, it is like feeling the storm, feeling the power of wind and lightning. Feel the landscape within you burning, the inner landscape burning and shattering. Go into the place of the shattering, let it break into a million pieces. What was before is now blowing up. Let your body shake and tremble. Allow your pain to exist, acknowledge it, honor it, have reverence for it. It is your teacher. It is bringing you into a place in your life that will change you forever. The experience of this pain is what will invite you to heal. Your desire to alleviate the pain will cause you to walk down a different path, to live in a different way than you have before. The first thing is do is to experience it. Go to where it resides, go inside the fire, don't turn away. Turn toward it, stop fighting it, don't resist it, allow it to be, breathe into it, and be with it. Look in the face of your pain. See whose face it is. Is she ten years old, twelve years old; is it the face of someone you have lost? Draw it. If it is very ugly and disturbing, it can be the face of a demon, the face of ugliness, the face of bitterness.

Now look into the darkness around the pain. See the emptiness around the pain. Feel its hollowness, feel the empty experience of being alone. Be in the space where pain resides. It is like being a star in the darkness of the night. You are bright, but in the darkness. It is like being in a rocket ship, you are weightless, formless, your consciousness is open and spacious, the pain is inside of it. From pain, all of a sudden, you are large, and there is an embodied three-dimensional space where the pain is. You are in a place where there is a death and you are about to be born. It is the moment before birth. Meditate on the pain. Allow it to have its own life, bear witness to it, stop resisting it. The second you allow pain to move around you, you see an opening in the rock. From the place of darkness, the void is the trigger to make art. You are not consumed with the pain anymore. When you go to the place of darkness, you let the pain move around. It is free in the world on its own; that is when you feel the void. To allow the pain to be on its own is difficult; you are attached to it, and it is hard to let it go. See your pain becoming a pain in the huge space. See it get relatively smaller, see that it matters less in your life, yet it is sacred and precious.

USING YOUR MIND'S EYE
TO TUNNEL FROM DARKNESS TO LIGHT

In your mind, picture a wonderful event when you felt powerful and strong. It could be a success, a moment of love, the birth of your baby, a spiritual vision. Take time and find one event. Go there deeply, go in between the moments. Slow time down, use all your senses, see it, feel it, smell it.

Now get protection, guides, helpers, and go to a place that is dark and has pain. It can be your illness, a past illness, a fear, a death of someone you love. With protection, go there, too; slow the time down and look at that event as long as you can.

Now imagine that there is a tunnel between the place of

great light and the place of darkness. Move through that tunnel from the dark place to the light place. Leave the place of darkness and go to the imagery of peace and beauty.

You can do this whenever you find yourself in your own darkness. You need not be afraid. You can stay there and examine what is dark for you, and you can, whenever you wish, leave and go back to your place of peace.

CHAPTER 5

Step Two: Go Elsewhere

A Shaman Appears

Lelana sits in her pottery studio next to an icy crystal-clear river in the mountains and tells us her story of healing:

> It was an awful time in my life. I had taken a new job and one of my first decisions was to hire an African American for a key position. The reaction of the people in this small Western town was swift and angry. I started receiving death threats; rocks were thrown at my house with notes on them. A fire was started near the house I was building. I became afraid. There was a real threat to my life and a constant possibility of violence.
>
> Then I became ill. The doctors found enlarged lymph nodes on my neck, and when they took one out, my vocal cords became paralyzed and I could not speak. They found more under my arms, and when they removed one, believe it or not, my left arm was paralyzed, too. I was weak and had no energy and now could not even communicate without

writing. I had gone from being someone very powerful and self-reliant to being someone on my back who could not speak and who was being subjected to death threats.

I went outside my house to an old tree. The tree had fallen in a huge storm. It lay down on the earth, long, heavy, and immovable. I sat on one of its smaller branches and rested there. It was the first time I had been at peace. The tree seemed to speak to me. Sitting on it, I learned it was ancient. It told me it had been there when Native Americans were the only ones here. They had had villages under this tree. It told me I was here for a reason, on this land. I had things to learn here. It told me I was on a pilgrimage. It was all happening for a reason, and I should pay attention to whatever I found around me. Later I found Jean Shinoda Bolen's book *Pilgrimages*, which was about being on a spiritual path. It reinforced the teachings of my ancient tree. This is what started my healing.

Then, for reasons I could not understand, I decided to make pots. If I could not speak, maybe I could make something that would speak. Since I could not use a wheel because of my left hand, I tried making slabs. The first slab immediately started forming itself into a man. It happened right in front of my eyes. I looked at the clay. It was becoming an ancient shaman, I could see that. It spoke to me like my tree. He said, "We are here with you. We are your guides. Listen to me and I will make you strong again." I could not understand it clearly, but that is what I thought when I looked into the eyes of the new figure that now faced me. "You will go on a pilgrimage," he said. "Your life will change. Take the stones that were thrown at you with hate notes on them and make them into prayer stones with prayers for healing on them. Paint animals on the stones, and prayers, and give them to children who are sick. Take your darkness and pain, and turn it into power and visions."

From that day, I felt that the ancient shaman was a presence around me always. He watched over me and helped me decide what to do. I healed physically. My arm could move again, and now I could speak again, too. I defended myself and spoke out, and the threats went away. My power returned. I gave one stone prayer bear to a mother of a little girl with cancer. The mother told me that the little girl would not give it up. She said she loved it, and it protected her.

I still work at my job, but now I also make these bears and make the clay shaman and give them to people. I know it helps them heal. I want my house to be a retreat for people to heal, too. The shaman told me that. He is with me always now. He is my healer.

Restory Your Own Life

In every story, the participants in the study described that after pain and darkness, they went inward or started "going elsewhere." By elsewhere, they meant away from the pain, suffering, and darkness. The research illustrates the universality of going elsewhere or inward for spiritual healing and elucidates the many ways people can do this.

The research found that it is not necessary to intentionally use the traditional spiritual techniques of meditation, prayer, or even guided imagery. Many of the participants did meditate or pray or use guided imagery, but in our study, the way people first were able to go elsewhere or inward was to be alone and to let something happen. Let a voice, a vision, a thought come by itself. Let yourself be creative, and do something in your life to make change. The participants made an English garden, went on a trip, made a pot, danced, played music, drew, or wrote. The important thing about going elsewhere was the value of opening up. We found that elsewhere is inside the inner world where the spirit can begin to be heard. When the participants were elsewhere, prayer or imagery came to them; they meditated on something that came to them in the elsewhere place they found. That deepened the experience.

The Pause Invites You

People who articulate going elsewhere find the theme of the pause within. Inside going elsewhere is a pause in people's lives that lets them start to heal. People find the pause in walks in the forest, in hospital rooms with nothing to do all day, in nature, or in wondering. It is as if their rhythm changed. There is a pause even within themselves. It is a place to consider for a moment before a choice is made. It is standing on the threshold.

We found a pause in each story. The pause seemed to be a critical occurrence. Often we found that the pause was not intentional. The participants did not necessarily want to do it, yet it happened naturally as they found themselves in a crisis. It was a surprise, an unexpected gift.

The pause is like an invitation. It asks you to do what you have never done, to consider a song, to remember the past, to see a vision in the doorway. The pause is the space in which your spirit first calls to you.

Dreams Take You from Your Outer Self to Your Inner Self

In this story, Phyllis uses dreams to deal with her most intimate and personal issues. She tells us about a split from her outer world to her inner world:

> I am a woman married to an attorney. My life is chaotic. My time is stretched beyond what is comfortable to me. The phone rings, I am trying to pay bills, to pay my taxes. I am exhausted at the end of the day. I don't know where my en-

ergy has gone. I don't have time for my friends anymore. I take antidepressants, I drink alcohol, I wish I had a lover.

My inner self is different. When I look out the window, like I am in this moment, I am just . . . blown away by the way the light is hitting the branch of that tree with the red leaves behind it. I am so moved by the way the light and dark are so incredibly illuminated. I wonder how can anything be that beautiful. I've gone away completely from my outer self in that moment.

There is a voice in my dreams. It is soft and sensual, it calls me and relaxes me. I fall into the moment with a deep sense of peace. I feel connected to myself. My dream world is sexual. I have many lovers. It is like I am in a mystical space where my breathing changes. It's softer, slower; the images are rich, colorful. The stories are complex and rich. It does not make any sense, but it does not have to. It is as if the boundaries between my inner and outer self are gone. It is like a dream, and I just float and fold one story into another. It keeps me alive.

Reclaim Your Dreamer Within

The split for the woman is between her ordinary life and her life as an artist and a dreamer. What she does is describe her rich dream world with its sensations and images and her ordinary world. Through her dreams and her art, she creates a mystical space within her life. Her way of seeing was her pause. She described it as an enchanted world within the physical space of carpooling, preparing meals, paying bills, and endless demands on her from her family. It helped her with her constant struggle in dealing with lifelong depression. In her dream world, she created a contrast. She said, "allowing the imagery to be free floating, pushed me into seeing my own luminosity."

Go Inward into Your Heart

Going inward is different for each person. Some participants called it going elsewhere; others called it going into their hearts. All of them started with who they were in their lives in the center of their fears and darkness. They started inside their pain. Their life problems or illnesses were the opportunities for them to heal, grow, and change.

Going inward also involves surprise and deepening. Most participants suddenly found themselves in another place. Then they deepened their inner state by staying there or going there over and over again.

Many of the people talked about going into the darkness and seeing images of their fear, woundedness, or illness that were frightening. It was essential that these images be seen and brought forth in their consciousness for them to begin to heal. Then, from the darkness, they went into a light. They became opened; they also were spoken to. The voices heard or images seen were of their own lives. They did not have to do anything. Suddenly the messages from the spirit would come, and they would get ideas, visions, dreams, jokes, or voices. The ways the spirit spoke to them were as varied as the people.

Go Elsewhere to a Safe Place

Melissa is now an artist-in-residence in an arts in medicine program. Previously, in her own life, she started making art to deal with the terrible darkness of sexual abuse. She said making her art took her elsewhere. She was the first participant in the research study to use that term. Melissa told us:

> I always used my creative fantasy play as the way of dealing with feelings of isolation. It was a way of dealing with something traumatic that happened to me as a child. It was a way

for me to take myself out of the world that was off balance. As a child, I needed to protect myself. It was about sexual abuse. So one of the ways I would protect myself was to create this inner world. My drawing was the way of illustrating this world and being in touch with it and being in a safe place.

Drawing became another way for me to see the beauty around this world. For a long time, I didn't remember the incidents that led up to that, but I knew I had always used creativity to create a different world, a different environment for myself. I would live there for a while when it wasn't safe. It was a way for me to communicate and be connected so these stories would come out. Through fantasies and drawings and illustrations, things would come out, and it was very positive. I felt very good about it.

When I did start to recall some of the issues that had happened in my childhood, I was able to face them through my drawings. I was dealing with the horrible darkness of childhood sexual abuse. The memories originally would come through dreams. My paintings were very dark because the dreams were very dark. The paintings were always of disempowerment, of being captured, of being dismembered. I really went into it. Being female, I took parts of me apart, and then I reassembled myself.

There was a point of divinity where I was able to cross thresholds and see myself as being part of the divine. It's taken years to really see. A lot of my attention went to the crucifixion and the symbolism of being crucified, feeling disjointed in life, not feeling like I fit. So the outlook also gave me a place where I was acceptable to fit in the way that I did fit.

"Elsewhere" for me was a beautiful place; it was like a Ferris wheel. It was a circus type of atmosphere where there were horses and animals. It was kind of like being my own character, being able to protect others. I felt like it was really important to protect others, probably because I didn't feel protected myself.

I would draw myself and I would be on a powerful horse. Or I would have lions that would lie down and be my powerful protectors. I could climb and I could fly. In my real life, too, I would climb trees, and I would stay up there and imagine myself being able to fly away. My drawings made a place for me to work out my problems and the dynamics within my family. There was a lot of anger and a lot of acting out on my part. Creativity gave me the place where I could make my characters work to create balance. Art gave me the opportunity to be right and then forgive myself for being wrong.

Melissa talks about dismemberment. The classic shamanic initiation in most cultures involves being taken down to one bone and put back together again in a sacred way. Melissa did just that. Going elsewhere led to re-creating herself anew as a beautiful sacred healer.

The process made her fall in love with art and herself. She wrote a book for children with leukemia about a kitten with cancer to help a child understand the experience of dying.

The Trigger Event Invites You

At some point, inside the pain, inside the darkness, something happens. A theme that emerges is the trigger event. In thinking about it, the trigger becomes an invitation to change. The trigger event could be a sunset, a swarm of butterflies, a workshop, a book. It could be a walk in the woods, a canoe ride paddling on a river.

For others, something inside their lives changed, so that they now were creative on a personal level, they now did something specific to heal. It is not clear that everyone received an invitation, but something happened that created a shift to initiate doing something or moving in a new direction. It is not always conscious. The person need not even know it happened, but there is always something that we would call the trigger of the invitation.

Act on Your Invitation to Heal

Many participants had the common factor of wanting all their lives to be something or do something. Then, when the invitation came, they responded quickly. A participant would say, "I always wanted to make pots, and never did," or "I always wanted to be a bicycle racer" and now in the illness they must. The imperative is balanced; there is nothing more to lose. It is as one person said, "In a lucid moment, I decided to abandon my fears of being a painter, something I had always dreamed of being yet had never given myself permission to be because I never felt good enough. This time I did not put so much pressure on myself to be 'good enough.' I just remembered I had always wanted to be an artist. At this time, I felt so devastated that the fear of inadequacy was minute compared to the painful loss I was experiencing. It was a combination of 'suddenly you do this because there is nothing left to lose, and you have always wanted this, and the darkness is there, and then I did something to change.'"

Remember Your Desires

The trigger is an event from the outside world that reminds you of who you are or who you could be. The trigger puts you in the past. It reminds you of who you were in moments of your deepest dreaming or beauty. It is a beginning of something else inside the death. It is a seed. The trigger is the glimmer of your own birth to become something different or new.

Suffering is a death of what you thought you wanted. The

suffering burns the landscape of your own life with its disappointment of what you wanted. You dream and go to the place you were the happiest in your life or to a place you held as a dream and never allowed yourself to go. In the deepest darkness, in the pause comes a blade of spring grass in the snow at dusk. It is the trigger to take a photograph, to begin to heal.

The Trigger Opens Your Heart

Seeing a sunrise, being in a powerful place, seeing great beauty, all can bring on the pause followed by the trigger and the opening of the heart. Even a moment as simple as seeing a child or being with something that evokes emotion, opens our hearts. The event can happen anytime and anywhere, even while you are watching television. It can happen when someone you don't even know speaks to you. You are ready to hear, you are ready to learn. All these events involve you seeing something greater than yourself. The events help you see yourself as part of the cosmic whole of life. You suddenly stand there and realize that there is a collective consciousness, like a vein you need to access within your life. Your soul within is freed and seen, your spirit illuminated.

Here is Michael's story about his mother:

> It happened when she was eighty-one years old. She had had an awful year. She had three failed angioplasties and now the bypass.
>
> She is in a bed in the intensive care unit after her coronary bypass surgery. Something has gone terribly wrong. Her lungs cannot move oxygen, and she is on a respirator and cannot speak. The machine breathes for her. She has been on it for a week. Her lung function is not improving. From her place in bed, her eyes look at me with terror and pain. It hurts me deeply. I see her the way she was and wonder

whether she will ever be the same. I try to relax her, I try everything, all my skills as a mind-body physician, but she cannot concentrate.

In desperation, I turn on the television to distract her. I find a show with two dancers embracing. They are doing a modern dance that is graceful and emotional. The music feels like spinning, the dancers whirl and touch and separate and touch again. They reach out for each other, and it looks as if each yearns for the other's touch. It is like a pulse, like the sea surging. Suddenly, my mother is captivated. She relaxes and looks at them and smiles for the first time. Her face softens and her breathing changes. She cannot talk because of the respirator, so she writes on a piece of paper on a clipboard. She writes one letter at a time with a faltering, trembling hand. It takes all her effort. She writes, "I remember dancing as a little girl." Each word is on a different line. Spaces that are full of emotion are between them. She closes her eyes and writes some more words, "In my mind . . . I now dance, too." She smiles a little, she is far away, she has gone to a place where she is at ease. I watch her go from panic and suffering to freedom and joy. In a moment, I relax, too, for the first time since her surgery. I can see that she is going to get well.

Getting attention through distraction is a common doorway to the inner world. Ken, a computer executive, told us that he went to work each day and became more and more depressed. He knew somehow he was not complete, he was not himself. Ken told us:

One day I went for a walk, all alone in a park. I felt like I was at the end of my rope. All I could think about was myself, all I could think about were all my problems. In my mind, all I could see was myself alone with nothing around me. My wife had left me, I was confused about myself. I felt depression and despair. Then I saw a woman who was living on the street. She walked up to me and looked directly into my eyes. I gave her some money. The next day I saw her again. It was spooky. I felt she was there to tell me something. I looked in her eyes and saw myself as a woman who did not have any money or food. She took my money again. I was stunned and deeply affected.

The next week, she came up to me, she asked me if she could have one hug. She said, no money, just one touch. I could not hug her, but I touched her and left. I walked a little distance away and I stood and cried. I felt space and time crack, I saw outlines of light and edges of time. The vision of myself changed before my eyes. I suddenly saw a vision of myself being a volunteer in a woman's shelter in a poor neighborhood.

Ken has done this volunteer work for two years. It is the most important and meaningful part of his life. He now knows much more about who he is and who he wants to be. He went elsewhere for just a moment, and when he was finished, he became alive again. Later he asked himself, who was she? Was she someone he had known in a previous life, someone sacred, an ordinary homeless woman? Was she Christ?

Reflections on Going Elsewhere

Going elsewhere is about movement; going elsewhere is the first movement from the darkness. It is a shift from being in pain to being out of pain. It is the threshold that starts us on our healing journey. Going elsewhere takes us into a different place that is timeless and spaceless. For many of us, this is our first experience of going into this space. Going elsewhere is our threshold into the inner world. It takes an opening up to get there.

Be Alone, Open, and Wait

Invite the pause to come. To do this, put yourself in situations where you are alone. Go for walks alone in nature. Watch sunsets, go to places in nature that have the energy of beauty. Let yourself be quiet. Let the cares and worries of the illness recede for even a moment.

To go elsewhere, you need only be aware that the invitation will come. The pause is the moment where it all stops. People are aware of moving forward, but not usually aware of stopping. Stopping is an absence. It is a not happening. Keep your eyes open, go in your daydreams. Be aware of your feelings. You do not need to do anything except honor going inward for it to happen. If you know it exists and wait, it will come to you. Just open and wait.

Daydream

Daydreams are an excellent way of going elsewhere. Fantasy, imagination, and building a rich world peopled with characters are all ways you can enhance going elsewhere. As one participant said, this is the place to be wild and free. If you can't do it in your outer life, do it now in your elsewhere. In this step, the message of your own life appears. You do not have to think of it or invent it. It comes to you. Going inward takes you away. It makes a new world that is safe. It makes a world full of beauty. There, something takes you and takes care of you. It is your spirit. It is Her or Him.

Create Protection

Going elsewhere is also about protection. If you need a safe place and protection for yourself or someone you love, call for it, and let it come.

Seek Your Invitation

The trigger can be sought. Go to watch sunsets, do workshops, read books, seek your own particular invitation. Coincidence and synchronicity are part of the experience of the trigger. A billboard can have a message for you, a television show, a license plate on a car you pass. The messages are everywhere; they all tell you what you need to heal. In going elsewhere, the first inner guides can appear. The guides and helpers can be people, real or imagined, animal, something in nature. In going elsewhere, you can see something greater than yourself. In going elsewhere, connections emerge, relationships form. Going elsewhere is a threshold to divinity.

Use Guided Imagery

USING YOUR MIND'S EYE TO FIND YOUR SAFE INNER PLACE

Make yourself comfortable. Go into your guided-imagery space. Let yourself relax, uncross your legs and arms, close your eyes, let your breathing slow down. Take several deep breaths. Let your abdomen rise as you breathe in and fall as you let your deep breath out. As you breathe in and out, you may feel tingling, buzzing, or relaxation. Let those feelings increase. You may feel heavy or light, you may feel your boundaries loosening and your edges soften.

Now let yourself relax. Let your feet relax, let your legs relax. Let the feelings of relaxation spread to your thighs and pelvis. Let your pelvis open and relax. Now let your abdomen relax, let your belly expand; do not hold it in any more. Now let your chest relax, let your heartbeat and breathing take place by themselves. Let your arms relax, your hands relax. Now let your neck relax, your head, your face. Let your eyes relax; see a horizon and blackness for a moment. Let these feelings of relaxation spread throughout your body. Let your relaxation deepen. If you wish, you can count your breaths and let your relaxation deepen with each breath.

Now see yourself at home in your house, doing something you usually do. Choose an activity that you don't really enjoy: paying the bills, cleaning, doing errands on lists. See yourself doing it, be there. Feel how your body feels. What do you see, what can you hear, smell, touch?

Now, for a moment, daydream. Let your mind wander to what you would really like to be doing right now. It can be a hobby, a sport, a walk outdoors, being with your family, being creative. Remember things you have done that you have really enjoyed. Remember dreams you have had that you have wanted to do but never done.

Pause for a moment and just rest. Concentrate on your breathing. Stay for a moment in the place after you breathe out. Stay in the place between breaths, and rest there and let your mind empty. Let it think about nothing at all. Stay in the pause as long as you would like.

Now come back to your daydream state. See whether you can glimpse a place you can go that is completely different from the place you are in now. It can be a fantasy land, a star in outer space, a magic garden, a workshop; it can be a place you have been or dreamed of, or one you invent or let come to you now. It can be in the forest, on a mountaintop, in a safe room in a beautiful home. Now look around you for who is there—are there people with you, teachers, family, animals? Are there tools, things to make art with? Let yourself make a place that is elsewhere, that is not where you are or live.

Go deeply into that place, see how your body feels there, smell the air, see what is near, hear the sounds. Spend time there. Let the images get richer, let more come to you, see more around you now. Feel how time is changed in this place. Time seems not to be moving here; space seems wider and more open. If you wish, you can invite protection to come to you here. You can invite a protective field or figures or animals that will protect you and be with you in this elsewhere place.

If you wish, you can let an inner workshop come to you. Let a place appear that is a place you can do things to heal. You can let healing medicines come, tools to build or make art, things that can heal your illness. They can be scientific or magical, real or imaginary. The workshop can be in nature or in a house.

When you are ready, return to the room where you are doing the exercise. First move your feet and then move your hands. Move them around and experience the feeling of the movement. Press your feet down onto the floor, feel the grounding, feel the pressure on the bottom of your feet, feel the solidity of the Earth. Feel your backside on the chair; feel your weight pressing downward. Now open your eyes. Look around you. Stand up and stretch, move your body, feel it move. You are back, you can carry the experience of the exercise outward to your life. You will feel stronger and be able to see deeper. You will be in a healing state. Each time you do the exercise, you will be more relaxed and be able to go deeper and be more deeply healed.

Suddenly you are on an adventure, a point of departure where you are inside the rose garden. Going elsewhere is going to the imagination within your imagination. Merge with roses, see them merge with you in a new place in your imagination. A guide within yourself reaches out, grabs your hand, and takes you there.

USING YOUR IMAGINATION
TO HEAL

Elsewhere is a window into your imagination, a place to daydream or to dream. To go elsewhere, sleep, remember dreams, allow your imagination to slip you into another three-dimensional consciousness that is different. Elsewhere can be a window in a hospital room, a journal where you become a character and let yourself slip into another time. It is a distraction, but it is deeper that that. Your mind takes you to something to pay attention to.

See the leaves on the branches and how the light is, see how the first snow looks; slip though that doorway into your imagination. Go to the moment inside the moment. See your bowl on your table, look through the eyes of a camera, see with a whole new frame. An external object of concentration lets you focus.

By saying a prayer, a chant, a mantra, or repeating "Hail Mary," you take your mind from one place and break the cycle of obsessive thoughts. You can exercise, dance, run, bridge to another side. That is a stepping-stone; the goal is to break the cycle, to make movement in meditation and go into that pause.

USING YOUR MIND'S EYE
TO HEAR AN INNER VOICE

Make yourself comfortable. Go into your guided-imagery space. Let yourself relax, uncross your legs and arms, close your eyes, let your breathing slow down. Take several deep breaths. Let your abdomen rise as you breathe in and fall as you let your deep breath out. As you breathe in and out, you may feel tingling, buzzing, or relaxation. Let those feelings increase. You may feel heavy or light, you may feel your boundaries loosening and your edges soften.

Now let yourself relax. Let your feet relax, let your legs relax. Let the feelings of relaxation spread to your thighs and pelvis. Let your pelvis open and relax. Now let your abdomen relax, let your belly expand; do not hold it in any more. Now let your chest relax, let your heartbeat and breathing take place by themselves. Let your arms relax, your hands relax. Now let your neck relax, your head, your face. Let your eyes relax; see a horizon and blackness for a moment. Let these feelings of relaxation spread throughout your body. Let your relaxation deepen. If you wish, you can count your breaths and let your relaxation deepen with each breath.

Imagine that you are on a walk. Let the place be somewhere you love: a forest path, the beach, the mountains, a favorite park. As you walk, feel the air on your face, feel the ground below your feet, smell the air, be there. Now find a place to rest. Look for a spot that sparkles, that attracts you, that calls out to you. It can be a log, a clearing, a rock, a bench. Sit down and rest a moment and pause. Look around you, see the Earth, the sky. Let feelings of immense peace come into you. Let your body relax deeply in the place of rest.

Look for a presence around you, which is a guide or helper. Look around you. If a guide appears or you can see it, let it come to you. Welcome it to you and listen to what it has to say. It will feel like your own thoughts but clearer and possibly with a different voice. It will feel like an insight, a creative thought, a message from your deep inner intuitive self.

Listen to the voice that appears to you. If you wish to respond, you can speak back in your thoughts and tell the voice what you are thinking.

When you are ready, return to the room where you are doing the exercise. First move your feet and then move your hands. Move them around and experience the feeling of the movement. Press your feet down onto the floor, feel the grounding, feel the pressure on the bottom of your feet, feel the solidity of the Earth. Feel your backside on the chair; feel your weight pressing downward. Now open your eyes. Look around you. Stand up and stretch, move your body, feel it move. You are back, you can carry the experience of the exercise outward to your life. You will feel stronger and be able to see deeper. You will be in a healing state. Each time you do the exercise you will be more relaxed and be able to go deeper and be more deeply healed.

Chapter 6

✸

Step Three: Find Your Own Turning Point

> Keep walking, though there's no place to get to.
> Don't try to see through the distances.
> That's not for human beings.
> Move within,
> but don't move the way
> fear makes you move.
> Today, like every other day,
> we wake up empty and frightened.
> Don't open the door to the study
> and begin reading.
> Take down a musical instrument.
> Let the beauty we love
> be what we do.
> There are hundreds of ways
> to kneel and kiss the ground.
>
> —Rumi

Why Do the Birds Sing in the Morning?

Yoshi, a Japanese engineer, a cancer survivor, tells us his story:

I was very sick. The doctor would not tell me what was wrong. In Japan, they do not tell you your diagnosis when you have cancer. One doctor finally came and said to me, "You have advanced kidney cancer. It is fatal. Get your things in order," then he turned abruptly and he left. He did not even look me in the eyes. My wife started crying. I started crying, too.

Then I hurt. I had hurt for months, and now with the news, I hurt even more. They kept me in the hospital but I did not feel better. They gave me medicines, and I became sicker and sicker. The doctor told me I would die soon. That was all right with me. I did not want to live anymore. I had nothing to live for. I was sick, and I hurt, and I was dying. There was no hope, they said that to me over and over again.

One day I left my room and went up to the roof. I went up because I was going to jump. I was desperate. There was nothing else I could do. I wanted to die with honor. Before I jumped, I paused. I looked out and saw the trees. I was in the center of the city, but still the trees were beautiful. And—I heard the birds sing. I gasped.

In my room, there was only the sound of the air conditioners and IV pumps. This was totally different. And I smelled the air. Even though I was in the city, the air was sweet smelling like a perfume, and as the soft wind blew, it seemed to come over me. In a moment, I felt like the wind was cleaning my body and even covering me with love. I opened my eyes wide and even wider, and I smiled with joy. I went directly downstairs. I took what was in my room, and I left the hospital against medical advice. It only took a moment.

STEP THREE: FIND YOUR OWN TURNING POINT

At home, I awakened each day before dawn. I had been an electrical engineer for a large company before I became ill. I could solve difficult technical problems, but they had no meaning for me now. I could not go back to work; this did not interest me. I was still too sick. I did not know what to do at home. The next day I awakened and heard the birds sing again. They were so beautiful, they were the most beautiful sounds I had ever heard. I was entranced. I went into that sound. I was taken into that sound. And then, I heard a voice from inside me like a loud thought. It said, "Why do the birds sing at dawn? What makes the birds sing?"

I was electrified. I ran to my workshop and got my tools. I thought, how could I find out why the birds sing? The next day I was up way before dawn. When it was still dark, I left my house and went out to the park where there were many more birds. I waited. My whole body was electrified in expectation for the first magnificent song.

It came. I gasped. It was so beautiful. Again, it was the most beautiful sound I had ever heard. I filled up with that sound. It echoed within me and opened up my body, and cleaned me out and made me feel whole again. It makes me laugh to think how my body felt. I do not know why that was. My mind was still racing.

Then one day, it did not matter to me so much why the birds sang. I realized I was so alive, my whole body tingled with energy, I was healthy. But more than that, I was new. My eyes were different. I saw beauty everywhere. I had a smile on my face all the time. Every bird was singing to me telling me I was on the right path. Each bird told me I was well again.

I knew I was healed. I was so happy. I was full of joy in every moment, so glad to be alive. I could not even believe how beautiful the world was. I could not believe I had lived all those years without feeling this excitement, seeing this beauty. I went to the doctor. He did tests and scans and told me my cancer was gone. He could not believe it. He said he must have had the wrong diagnosis, he said it was impossible for me to be cured from that cancer.

I was a totally new man. My enthusiasm overflowed. I loved sounds so much then that I started learning to play the cello. It was as beautiful to me as the song of the birds at dawn. Just touching the cello brought a huge smile to my face. It filled me with joy and energy to play the beautiful songs I learned. I was so happy. I wanted to share my experience, to tell everyone about what had happened to me.

Be Creative

Creativity has a forward movement. It has a focus and a rhythm. The participants focused on the creative process—on their visions, drawings or music or dance—not the pain, until they did not feel the pain anymore. The creative process helps patients see their spiritual experience more deeply. It is the only way some participants could see what was happening in the world of their unconscious. For some people, the spiritual experience was enough. They needed only to see the swarm of butterflies as the face of God. For others, they needed to find out why the birds sing in the morning. They found it helpful to go deeply with a process into their spiritual visions or quest.

The Process of Creativity Is Healing

This theme is the process itself, the actual participation in creative work. It allows you to deal with your own experiences of pain and suffering or to face death in a way that is continuous and gets your attention over time. Creativity in any form allows you to engage in a process where you are embodied in an interaction with yourself.

We have found that whether you see a vision of the face of

God or want to find out why the birds sing in the morning, your involvement in a creative visionary space is a key element. Creative processes allow you to take the inner image of the vision and see it more clearly and bring it out. If you have an image of a sacred garden, the image is made real when you garden, tell us your story of the sacred garden, or paint a picture of a garden. When the woman saw the butterflies as the face of God, she took that vision and made it a story that included her as beautiful; she framed the vision within her life and moved forward with the new vision as part of her.

The creative act starts differently for each person. Some participants already were gardeners, some were artists. Some had been creative, some had never done creative work before. It is in the process of being creative that they change. The discovery of creativity is a turning point. The change begins with darkness, a void, then goes elsewhere. Finally, there is the trigger to enter a creative process of healing.

They go into it, into intuition, instinct, body sensations, to move deeper, to self-discovery. They emerge in a new place where there is now light, as well as darkness. There is life, as well as death. They can feel the wind in their faces again.

The Creative Spirit Emerges

You go from the outer world to the inner world. You move into a realm of who you are, more than physical, more than emotional. You begin to be immersed in spirit. You make a critical shift in consciousness. The creative process is a fully embodied process where the participants told of being immersed, going with the flow, trusting what emerged, and being healed by the beauty itself. Inherent in the process of creativity is an absorption and a movement. Creativity involves an act, an actual creation, of making something. Whether it is a story, form and lines, or a movement or a sound, you do something in the world. You move into the flow of energy, move into the spiral of your own life force. This takes you from within to the world outward. You take the energy from your own life force, spiraling in and spiraling out.

Healing Images Come from the Unconscious

You are hypersensitive in a focused way. That is how the inner artist takes you to your inner healer. Your focus on creativity puts you in an altered state that frees your inner physiological resources.

For healing, the change in physiology is the secret link, the tangible link to the body, to how the human creates itself. A baby is created and grows without the mother's conscious participation. He or she grows inside, hidden. The growth is unconscious, it comes from deep in the universe's past. Creativity, too, comes from your unconscious; it, too, emerges from deep within the universe's past.

Open Your Mind to Something New

The turning point is an openness of mind. It is the place where the initial vision is allowed to grow and become rich. It can be as simple as staying with a vision and allowing it to happen or as complicated as making seventy-one paintings of a bridge and water to heal yourself of Hodgkin's disease. It can be an activity or a state of mind of creativity and imagination. Our participants did all kinds of things that took them deeper into their visions with a creative process. Walks, gardening, humor, and helping others were common. Making web sites, writing joke books, performing rituals, saving a river, and walking in nature were used by our respondents. Prayer, retreats, making art, meditating, performing body work, using guided imagery, doing yoga or Qi Gong, and travel—all were used. The activities were about deepening the practice. They were spontaneous and not usually known before they happened. They were not done by an expert, conducted as a career in order to succeed. They were done to heal. They were often simple and not technical. A journal was written in the simplest book.

Throughout all of history, when people suffered, they did things to change. In the book of saints, the people all had the visions in great suffering. They became saints in adherence to the faith in their own spiritual life. They had faith and a tremendous trust in the process. Faith, hope, charity, love, compassion, and thankfulness were all the basis of the spiritual traditions. Our participants discovered these things by themselves in the process of Spirit Body Healing.

Reclaim Your Writer Within: Journaling

Keith, an artist and teacher, wrote a book about healing himself after his wife died of cancer. Here is a journal entry about her death:

> Debbie died at 2:15 in the afternoon on February nineteenth, nineteen hundred and ninety. The night after her death, I had the most extraordinary and vivid dream. I was in a hospital being restrained by three doctors. They were pleading with me not to go into Debbie's room. They said her body had decomposed, and if I saw her in that condition, it would leave me with a very unpleasant final vision. I became angry and pushed them aside and told them I had to see her.
>
> I ran to her room and opened the door. Debbie was reclining, unclothed, on her side, in the way of the Odalisque in the painting by Ingres. Her body was radiant, full and perfect. Her hair shone like golden threads, and her lips and cheeks were pink and glowing. I stared at her in amazement. The doctors were wrong. She was perfect. I went to her

bedside and sat down. Her eyes were closed, and her hand hung limp. I embraced her, and as I did, her chest heaved, her eyes opened, her lungs filled with air and she became alive. My heart stopped and my eyes welled with tears of joy. Debbie looked up at me and said, "Keith, I am not alive."

I paused and then asked her, "Is it good or bad where you are?" She looked at me and rolled her eyes in the way she would when I had said something really dumb. She said, "Good and bad do not apply here."

I said, "Well is it okay? Are you okay?"

Debbie's lips tightened and her eye squinted as if to say, let me think about that one. Then slowly she nodded her head and said, "Yes, it's okay, but I need some time to get used to it."

I held her shoulders and looked into her face and asked, "Debbie, when I die, will I be able to be with you?"

She said, "Yes."

Her eyes then closed, and her body went limp again. I panicked and ran into the corridor and began a desperate search for the doctors. The halls were deserted. I decided to go back into Debbie's room, but I could not find my way. I began opening doors in the corridor, but all the rooms were empty. I awoke sitting up in bed.

A poet speaks about the threshold of being: Through the brilliance of an image, the distant past resounds with echoes, and it is hard to know what depth these echoes will reverberate to. The phenomenon of the poetic image when it emerges into the consciousness is a direct product of the heart, soul, and being of humanity.

Before her illness, Keith had been an art teacher at a community college. He had never used his art to heal. He used journals, poems, drawings to deal with his wife's death. With this wonderful work, he became a healing artist. Keith wrote this poem about dealing with her death:

Mourning Sickness

mourning sickness
growth and change
dance this dance
with loss and pain
see the furred petaled and winged world
eating destroying being born and unfurled
searing fearful horrific and blind
peaceful potent serene and sublime
testing, testing
are you ready to conceive
to deal with
what is dealt
from the magician's sleeve
you are pregnant with God
you are great with soul
giving birth to yourself
is life's greatest goal
do not be stillborn again.

Keith is now married again and has children. His grief helped him give birth to his new life.

Reclaim Your Dancer Within

To dance for healing is about moving. With every movement, you embody the creative fire within the dance; your body has a life of its own. Within every one of us is a dancer. The dancer within us is the seducer, the seductress, the one who creates a healing spiral around us. If we are seduced enough, we move into the dance and are part of the movement of healing. If you are a nurse, a mother, a person who is ill, you start to dance from room to room. You are in the midst of tasks, and if, within all of this, you close your eyes and see yourself as a dancer, you see that you live in the dance of your own life. Instead of rushing from place to place, you shift your body's perspective. All of a sudden, you see yourself dancing through your own life. You become graceful and beautiful by a deliberate conscious act, an intention.

Through this possibility of dancing at any moment in our lives, dancing in any moment, we can see ourselves in total grace and beauty. In the dancing moment, there is spontaneity and fun. You can move in any way you want to, you dance and twirl, allow yourself to stretch, to open. Embody movement that is natural and flowing like a river. Your movements become art, they become a dance.

Dance heals by spiraling us down inside ourselves to a center where tensions are released and there is a freedom and spaciousness. To dance is to harness the fire inside your belly, which moves you. You are always in movement, you go inside where you are held in place and then move outward. You thrill to the momentum and the movement that frees you. You feel the wind as you move; it livens your senses. You twirl, you move, you feel your spirit's rhythm.

Feel Your Healing Energy Move As You Dance

Dance is a vehicle for emotional expression, an opportunity to embody emotion. To use dance as a way to spirit, you can dance an image of a scene, become a forest, an animal. Choose your own image, and dance it for another person. Then you can dance together. You can dance a moment of pain or illness. You can use healing dance as a way to connect to someone. You can become sensitive to how you move, and how another person moves. You move with that person and let the person push on your hand. You connect with the essential energy each person has inside.

Each person has a specific energy, a way of moving. You connect with it and harness it for healing. You start to move, you get into your energy, you get tingly, alive. Your cells vibrate, you tap into your own energy source. As you move, you feel the imagery within you become real, alive. If you imagine you are a tree, you move your arms as branches and you feel like a tree. When you dance with someone who is ill, your very movements flow to them, lifting them, or caressing them, and sending them your healing energy.

The imagery does take you into the dance. What is healing is the actual dance. Your body and spirit become one and really free. The energy of the experience becomes palpable. Writing, painting, song, and dance are like a continuum that goes from thought to movement, embodying the creative process. In dance, you are truly embodied, translating thought and emotion into movement. When you get cells moving, neurotransmitters and endorphins are flowing. You express any fluidity that you are capable of. You let go of whatever is tense. Your body leads you where it wants to be naturally.

How does it feel to experience creative dance, to be within the creative fire? This is one dancer's experience of healing herself with dance:

> As I go deep into the sacred spiral, as I fall deeply into the center of the spiral of my whirling dance, through my love and my dreams of creation, I fall into the center of the spiral nebula, and this is what I see: There is a moment where I am one with the world around me, with the room or place I am in. In that moment, magic happens. The creative process, the same process that fuels the universe, that causes stars to be born, nebulae to come, babies to be born, also heals me. I get a feeling of deep peace. My body is calm and electric at once. I see everywhere. I am connected to everything.

What actually happens in this moment of dance as magic? We believe it is the same process in which the universe is formed from the dream, when matter is formed from thought. Just as the universe is creative by making stars, you are creative by dancing. As you explore the dancer within, you'll connect to the deepest moments in your life. It is this deep place of being where you'll find inner peace.

Reclaim Your Painter Within

Rouault described a philosophy of art: "In the domain of painting, we must start from the center, at the very heart of the circle from where the whole thing derives its source and meaning: and we come back again to that forgotten and outcast word, the soul. Paintings like this are a phenomenon of the impassioned soul. In the resonance we hear in the art, in the reverberation we speak it, it is our own. The reverberations bring about a change of being."

Use Art as Your Spiritual Practice

The theme that art resolves inner conflicts is basic to art and healing. The theme of art being a way to resolve opposites is also interesting. Artists speak of art as a profound spiritual practice in itself, an embodiment of spiritual truth ritually full in its result. For patients with cancer, art resolves the opposites of life and death. When cancer patients make art, they can see themselves healing in a miracle that may be different from what the physician had told them would happen.

Being Directed by Art

Denise, a woman with chronic fatigue syndrome, talks about healing herself by painting; each movement in her art is directed:

My paintings entered me into a very deep healing process. They were powerful, a powerful door to help me conquer a virus that had taken over my body. I was directed to paint each color, each image, each pattern, from a different voice within, a part of me that was fighting for my life. Every painting in the series took me on a unique journey that informed me of another part to the healing process. The painting and I became one until it was time to move on. I was moved by my art through an illness that forever changed my life.

The following story was taken from Rose Montgomery-Whicher's dissertation of the lived experience of drawing. It exemplifies the experience of how a drawing becomes alive and speaks to the artist:

Now I draw in response to the drawing, as well as in response to my sister sitting opposite me. The drawing, as the saying goes, now has a life of its own. It is as if it is no longer I who draw but the drawing itself that draws my attention to what it needs. I heed its demands and follow its leads; the shadow under her mouth wants to extend itself just a little to the left. I draw the extension. I continue in this manner until my drawing looks up at me and says, "Yes, I am finished, you can stop now."

Take a Journey to Self-love

As both a patient and an artist, Darlene used her creative resources and empowered herself to become deeply involved in her own recovery from chronic pain. Diagnosed with fibromyalgia—a chronic, painful condition that had severely disabled her to the point that she became wheelchair-bound and severely depressed—she began a series of seventy-two drawings, which she refers to as "The Journey." The first painting was titled simply *Pain*. After she became engaged in the drawing process, the colors, patterns, and symbols took on significance to her, and her drawings began to guide her in new directions. She drew out her pain.

Make Meaning from Despair

Kendra tells her story of making sculpture to heal her cancer:

> An artist asked me to make a sculpture on my experience of cancer. Make art out of cancer? Snatch meaning from the jaws of meaninglessness? We had many conversations. The point of departure for this sculpture was a memory. I was lying in the bed in a cloud of pain a few days after surgery for an adenoid cystic carcinoma of the ear canal, a rare neoplasm. I was drawn up into the cloud as it opened into a tunnel, leaving the noise of the hospital behind. The pain dropped away, and I had the strongest sense of peace of my mother's presence. I had a choice to make: Do I accept or do I struggle? The choice was a totally free one. I felt reassured that either choice was suitable for me. Struggle was the one I chose. I drifted back down the cloud tunnel. The hospital chatter and the bedside pain re-emerged.

Cecelia shares her story of dealing with breast cancer through art. She describes her process:

> I have to say that I didn't plan what the pieces were; they just came from my unconscious. There were times when I would try to manipulate what I was going to do. It did not feel right, and I couldn't allow myself to do it. I discovered that if I just let go and just let my unconscious mind, my spiritual part of me, take over, I made the best art. If I just listened to

that and heard it and saw it, that these wonderful pieces were created. During the whole process of making the pieces, I wasn't quite sure with each one what they really were about. As I made them, by the time I finished the piece, it really became clear what it was. I then understood what aspect they represented.

I spent a lot of time walking by myself. I did not go on the walk with the intention of coming up with some answers, but I just went on a walk to free my mind of clutter. It was amazing that these things occurred—these revelations would just come up. They would pop up and I would write them down. I kept a journal, but it was very informal. Eventually, at the end of three years, I had made eleven pieces. After I had finished the eleven pieces, another revelation occurred. I saw that in the beginning, all my pieces were very large. It was looking at the whole philosophical aspect of breast cancer and the parts that were really not very scary. As time went on, at the very end, all my pieces became smaller and smaller. Those were the pieces that were really about the difficult part—that I might die—and all of these very, very scary things.

It had been eighteen years, and I was just so emotionally drained from that. It was at that point that I really felt that I was healed. I had gotten over the trauma, and I was beyond it, and I could just let go of that part that I had dealt with for so long. It was kind of like starting all over again—I mean I felt really free. The other way of looking at it was in the beginning, these large pieces represented this huge enormous hole in me. As I began to make the pieces, the hole kept getting smaller and smaller and smaller until it finally just closed up and I was healed.

Making art can involve making a series, making one image, then another, then another. As you make them, you go from one place to another—from large to small, from bleeding to whole, from water to bridge. In making a series, you get deeper. You create movement. It happens over time. The images change. Healing occurs because something gets resolved, so you move on.

Make Shamanic Art to Heal

Christiane has made body castings of people with heart disease, organ transplants, asthma, and other diseases. Each piece of art shows the person who is ill and makes the artwork serve as a transformation that gives the person a new view of her- or himself or the illness. Her sculpture is a new type of studio art, art made with the intent to heal another person. Christiane's process of sculpture is simple, elegant, and extraordinary all at once. People are often referred to her by physicians. She talks to the person who comes to her, and together they see a vision. The vision comes out of the simple sharing of stories of the lived experience of the person's illness. She glimpses the subject of the piece with the person, and together they see the spirit of what the person will transform into.

Then Christiane makes a body casting of the person. The piece of art embodies the transformation, the art is the transformed form and is believed to help make the process of transformation happen. By participating in the making of the transformation and by looking at the finished piece, the person becomes transformed. In the process, Christiane herself is transformed, too. She is now the embodied shaman, the one who sees the transformation, manifests it, and makes it happen. She is powerful, and her process is real. She is an artist-healer, a contemporary shaman, an exceptional woman.

Use Creativity As the Journey

Creativity is a journey that takes place over years. The creative process happens over a long time period, especially when a person does something grand or makes a series of works. Patients were creative through the whole process of healing, during and after treatments, in and out of the hospital. Participants used many different kinds of media in the long process of healing. The process happened over time. Days went by with the works being made, then there were days in between with no creativity.

Turn to the Garden

In the darkness, Nancy glimpsed an English garden. While getting chemotherapy, her oncologist talked to her about English gardens he had visited. She closed her eyes and dreamed. The darkness of chemotherapy turned to spinning flowers, to whirling colors, to peace.

When she was going elsewhere, she went to her dream gardens. Her invitation came from the unexpected place of her oncologist. Then she saw it everywhere. A woman at the market in her little village was an expert in antique roses. A shop in the next town carried many varieties. A slide show, a book—all were triggers.

The turning point, however, was her trip. Nancy planned it even when she was most ill. It was so important to her it was all she would ask her doctor. "Can I go on my trip to England?" and she bought books, did research, made hours of phone calls. She asked friends to make the hotel reservations—she planned which gardens to visit.

The next step on returning home was to plan her own English garden. A dear friend did the master plan. He built a classic gate and brought it over to her when she was too sick even to come out of her room. The woman in town who was an expert in antique roses appeared and helped her choose plants and place them.

Save the Earth to Heal

Dominique, a depressed and ill woman, took a walk next to a river and had a vision. She followed the vision, and her turning point was to clean up a river. She tells us this story of healing herself and her sacred river:

> Six years ago, I had my vision of "The Great Cleansing of the Rio Grande." Every month, on the seventeenth, I make my way through the trickle, trash, disrespect, and despair, filling up uncountable garbage bags, walking towards the great river, sending her energy.... Listening, learning to hear the silences, making an art prayer.
>
> As I walk—picking up one can from the river then another on and on doing countless rosaries—what matters is the depth of my relationship with the river, my awe [at] the miracle of her beingness, her creativity, our oneness, our moment, our cocreation.
>
> The walking dictates the story. The walking is a dance. The walking dance is syncopated by gestures—picking up a can from the river, then another. Gifts are bestowed (found objects, encounters, or soul imprints). Walking motion, water, life... it is body and mind dancing through heart. The walking in the river is the gift—gift received, gift to be shared.
>
> The river flows, the river flows, there is no stopping her. All rivers are connected; I have learned that frequenting my river. They feed each other, or connect though currents of invisible energy, memory carriers of the interconnection of all life. People function in the same way. One way to activate these currents is through ritual. Rituals are icons of connections, they are the art of our lives.
>
> Rivers never seem to stop. They are weavers weaving silver filaments into the tapestries of life, and life well lived

brings the fruit of oneness and love—that, she taught me. Our hearts are open, we are heartists.

Reflections from the Turning Point: Follow Your Passion to Your Turning Point

Spinning, turning, doing, this is the step of making change. From wherever the person was before, this is the place where manifestation grows and deepens. The turning point is the step of manifestation. If humor was what came out of going elsewhere, now is the time to collect jokes, to write them down, to give speeches with jokes in them. If, on her walk, a woman saw a fiber shield, now is the time to make the first one, to get the materials together and to see what happens. If hiking was the opening, now is the time to plan for a hike each day, to research new trails, to go on a trek to Nepal.

Creativity as healing is an opening. It is about changing your life for real in real time. The processes include imagery, visions, dreams, walks, retreats, gardens, travel, making art. They are all the doorways to change. Out of the unconscious, images appear from the depths to heal. Whatever you do gives you images and visions from your spirit to heal you.

Let your energy and enthusiasm propel you forward. It is about movement, so encourage it to move. As your vision grows, make a story of it, and put yourself in as the hero or heroine. If you are making an English garden, see yourself as the woman with breast cancer who is creating a mandala garden to heal. Restory your life as the man who heard the birds sing, the man who learned to play the cello, the man with testicular cancer who went on to win the Tour de France bicycle race.

Turning point is a process. Embody it, feel it, do it over time. Let it grow as a series with change and movement. With each piece in the series or each new act done, based on the one before, let yourself be taken deeper and deeper by the process.

Use Guided Imagery

USING YOUR MIND'S EYE
TO FIND YOUR ARTIST WITHIN

Make yourself comfortable, uncross your legs and arms. Close your eyes. Let your breathing slow down. Take several deep breaths. Let your abdomen rise as you breathe in and fall as you let your deep breath out. As you breathe in and out, you may feel tingling, buzzing, or relaxation. Let those feelings increase. You may feel heavy or light, you may feel your boundaries loosening and your edges soften.

Now let yourself relax. Let your feet relax, let your legs relax. Let the feelings of relaxation spread to your thighs and pelvis. Let your pelvis open and relax. Now let your abdomen relax, let your belly expand, do not hold it in any more. Now let your chest relax, let your heartbeat and breathing take place by themselves. Let your arms relax, your hands relax. Now let your neck relax, your head, your face. Let your eyes relax; see a horizon and blackness for a moment. Let these feelings of relaxation spread throughout your body. Let your relaxation deepen. If you wish, you can count your breaths and let your relaxation deepen with each breath.

Now see yourself in your own home, in a place that is purely yours. It can be your studio, office, workroom. If you do not have your own place at home, find the place you are most comfortable. You can make a place that is yours right now—let one appear; it can be a real place at home or one in an imaginary room or area that does not exist right now.

Let yourself sit in a comfortable area in your own place. Sit in a position that is best for you, yoga style, on a chair, reclining. Now go into your own body, go into the center of your heart. Rest there a moment. Now from the center of your own heart, invite your inner creative person to come to you. In your imaginary space, take a spin, a twirl, spin around. Let your relaxation deepen, and as you breathe in and out, let a highly creative person you have always wanted to be emerge from deep within you. It can be an inner artist, a writer, painter, dancer, musician—an inner gardener, an inner scientist, an inner dreamer. Be open to whatever appears, do not judge or worry. Let the inner creative person come to you from far in your past—he or she may have been hidden for years. Did you paint as a child, did you river raft, did you keep a journal?

Welcome the inner creative person to your life. You can speak to this person, thank her or him for coming, ask a question. Now ask this person to start the first activity. Ask the person to make a painting, start a garden, find out something you always wanted to know. Watch as the person works—it is you, you know. It is your inner creative person at work.

Let yourself and the creative person merge. Let the person come up into your body and let the person's hands be your hands. After all, the person is you. Now let the person's activity merge with you. You become the painter, the gardener, the explorer. Welcome your inner artist.

Now come back to yourself. As you start to move your arms and legs, remember what your inner creative person did and who the person was. See out of the person's eyes. This is who you are, your turning point. Say to yourself, I am an artist. I am a creative person, I am a gardener. This is an important step in your getting deeply involved in what you have always wanted to do: to heal.

CHAPTER 7

Step Four: Slip through the Veil

The Magnolia Blossoms' Veil

Laverne, a woman who has breast cancer, tells us this story:

> I was in my oncologist's office to get the results of my CT scan. I waited for him to come into the room. I had done this many times before in the three years I had had breast cancer. He came in and looked dour. He said, "I am so sorry. The scan is not good. Your cancer has spread throughout your lungs." He said he would go and read the film himself and then talk to me later this afternoon about my treatment options.
>
> I did not understand what all this meant completely, but I was shocked and numb. I did not know what to say or do. So I decided to take a walk with my husband in the arboretum. He was silent, glum; he could not even look in my eyes. He looked like his world had come to an end. We walked slowly together through the beautiful plants.
>
> The magnolia was in bloom. I have never really looked at a magnolia before; I do not grow them in my garden. I

looked at the first one. It was open, wild, exuberant. Its colors were sensual and drew me in. It was like an invitation. The purples, blues, reds, whites carried me. The soft moist texture sucked me into the center of the blossom where I was in a new place.

In there, I was simply taken care of. The voice of the magnolia was saying, "I am the Earth, feel my body. I am the odors, smell me. I am the moisture, taste me. I am the new exuberance, the flowering. My blossoms are the birth of beauty. My blossoms are the birth of color, I am the birth of a new world. Come into me, do not be afraid. Come into my sensual tropical verdancy."

It all took place in a moment. I cannot even guess how long it took in real time. Even though it was only a moment, I was now different. I felt somehow that I could handle this. I felt grounded deeply in the Earth. I felt I was part of something much greater than only my life.

I called my husband. I said to him, "Look honey, look at the magnolia. Look at its shapes, its colors, its openness, its beauty. Look at how it is curved, how the purple flashes out of the whiteness. Look at how each blossom is shaped. Look how this one is different from that one. See how each type, each variety is subtly different."

He stopped and paused. He changed. He looked at me, not the magnolia. He saw me. He looked directly at me, deep into my eyes. I could see that he saw my beauty. I could see that he saw my bravery, my spirit. That was deeply healing to me.

Slip into Enchantment

Slipping though the veil is the step where you slip into a world of enchantment. You are within your ordinary world, and you see a flower, write a poem, and then you are on the other side.

It is as if you were on the side of ordinary reality and then you move across to the other side, where everything is extraordinary.

Slipping through the veil is like going elsewhere, but it is going deeper into the spiral. Remember, the process of Spirit Body Healing is not linear. Slipping through the veil is like a return to going elsewhere, but now you are completely taken. Now you are on the other side and can stay there longer and in a fuller way.

Slipping through the veil is like being inside your reality. It is being in a deeper place inside your own body. People tell us that their own body feels fuller, their sensations are heightened. They are inside reality in a more palpable way. Slipping through the veil is like merging. In the foregoing story, Laverne merges with the magnolia flower. It is like a new dimension to the fullness of life. You feel the pulsating of your own body, you feel your own breath, your own skin. You become beautiful. Even in deep crises, you know it will be all right. The world is not superficial anymore. You are experiencing something authentic. You are experiencing authentically who you are. It is as if you can feel, see, and know more deeply than you did before. When Laverne slipped into the magnolia, she knew she was beautiful on the other side. When she merged with the magnolia, she felt she could handle her difficult situation.

Feel the Spaciousness Inside

As you slip through the veil, suddenly, you are within your own body in a place of spaciousness. This is the place where the light appears and stays. The process deepens; you can see much more here. One person had a dream of God, another saw the Buddha, another felt an experience of enlightenment. They can slip through the veil and glimpse angels, God, saints, grandparents, or ancestors. They find themselves suddenly curled up in God's hands, held and comforted. A woman sees a rock open and fill with light.

Slipping through the veil is the place of opening. It is where the participants move out of pain to see their spirits dance. Slipping through the veil, they experience a shift, a new world appears. People see or hear messages of reassurance, beauty, and brightness. It is as if their own body, mind, and spirit would heal in and of themselves, if a person would open up and let it happen.

The veil is the pivot, the hinge on which your healing revolves. It is the center of the healing process. On one side of the veil is pain and darkness. Then there is the pause, the trigger, creativity as a turning point. Then you truly go through the veil into spirit.

Go into Mystical Enchantment

On the other side, all is different. You are now in a new world. On the other side of the veil is a place of enchantment, where you are fully elsewhere. You are now in compassion, light, creativity, flow, a process that carries you forward into a new life. You are in a life where you are part of something, one with the Earth. You begin the journey where you are creatively doing something to heal yourself, others, and the Earth, and that puts you in a position to teach and transform. You are in relationship to society, to the social order. You have transcended yourself and are now healing others.

This is a healing of the whole person and of your life. You go from being in pain to being the hero, from being in darkness to being in light and sharing that light with others. You go from isolation and fear to being a powerful, self-integrated healer in the culture.

The rest of the steps in the process of Spirit Body Healing take place on the other side of the veil. They take place in enchantment, in energy, in transcendence.

Take a Shamanic Journey

Jack is a dancer who has had AIDS for ten years. He started dancing at a workshop, where he drew a life-size image of his body and danced the forms he drew. He told us this story:

> I started with scribbles. It was completely mysterious to me what would happen next. But I was entranced. Right away, I loved moving. I closed my eyes, and I would swing back and forth. It was amazing to me how open and physical I could be. Then I started leaping on the huge dance floor, and then I was down on the floor rocking like a lonely ship, all alone on the sea. I became frightened. But I also became one with the sea.
>
> I heard a sound come out of me like the roar of the ocean. I felt waves break over me. And then, like a wave breaking, I started roaring like in the storm. It was like a giant explosion, a thunder clap. I started weeping. Years of sorrow, grief, darkness, and confusion started me weeping. It felt like the demons were rolling out of me. I had broken down, finally, totally, and completely. I was totally uninhibited.
>
> But inside the violent storm was another part of me that was perfectly still. I discovered a peace and calmness inside the storm. It was like the water was flowing both ways: into a violent powerful storm and into a place of peace. It felt like I had slipped into the water and was one with the water. Finally, my weeping stopped, my body was exhausted. I felt deeply cleansed by the water of my own imagery. Now it was like the storm had passed. Things were like they should be in my life. A place appeared inside of me that was totally natural. I could honor the natural flow finally and let things be the way they were. When the demons showed themselves in the storm, I knew I had nothing to fear. The fears were my soul friends.

He worked with people with AIDS and other dancers to teach and heal. The experience connected him to others in a deeper way.

Do Real Magic: A Communion

Slipping through the veil is also about attention, about a one-pointedness of mind. The experience of riveting attention is a characteristic of healing common to many participants. Gina tells a story of working with a young child in a burn unit:

> This is probably the most extraordinary experience I have ever had about attention. I was in a burn unit in Russia with Patch Adams, on a trip he runs to bring clowns to children who are ill. There was a child who had been burnt on three quarters of his body. His whole back, from the top of his neck all the way down to his feet, was burned, so I never saw his face. He had just been debrided and had been wailing for 45 minutes when I walked in.
>
> I felt instantly that I should draw for him. I leaned the drawing pad across the bed, and I only saw the side of his face, and I started to draw. As soon as I began drawing, I could feel his attention riveted on the line. There was no separation between me and the line and the child. I drew very, very slowly, and a moon emerged and a little clown dancing on the corner of the moon. As I was drawing, the child stopped crying. He was catching his breath, and within 10 minutes, he was not crying. My hand was moving, and I could sense his eyes. I could see his eyes on the slow motion of my hand making every line. Patch Adams leaned over to me, and he said, "Whatever you are doing, don't stop—that's real magic."

Inside of one moment, a bridge has been created between one human being and another. The child follows the artist across the veil. The line captures the child's sense of sight, the child is pulled in, it is a meeting. Their eyes are focused on the same exact place: the place where the point of the pencil meets the paper. It seems ordinary, but it is the place where one person connects with the other's experience. It seems as though you can take it for granted, but it is the doorway. It happens with drawing, dance, song. It is a communion of two people coming together:

> The child and I were breathing together because I was very close to his body. I was leaning over him, and I could feel his breathing, and I could sense this synchronizing happening. As I drew very, very slowly, his breathing became steady and slow, and I synchronized my breathing to his breathing. I just kept drawing at this pace so that the drawing unfolded and the breathing became very meditative and very deep and very quiet.
>
> His mother had been in a total panic because her child who had been burned horribly was screaming and inconsolable. She also changed. You could feel her unwinding, she started to breathe deeply, you could hear her breathing. Then everybody's breathing in the room changed—even the child in the bed next to us; his breathing changed, too. The mother could leave the room, and I just stood there drawing, and the child unwound.
>
> I just drew and drew. I drew three pictures, and we taped them all on the wall across from the bed, where he was looking, so he could see them every time he opened his eyes. Because of the way I was leaning over the bed, I was in the most uncomfortable position I could imagine. I could feel all my muscles cramping, yet I was in this place, it was like bliss. It was being in the presence of something extraordinary.

Breathe in Oneness

Oneness can go as far as a synchronization of breathing. In our study, this was unusual and probably due to Gina's experience with meditation. The riveting of attention is an experience shared by many patients. The patient moves across the veil from an experience of suffering to a place of becoming totally absorbed. We have also seen this with dancers and patients; the attention is riveted by a patient watching a scarf moving. The patient's eyes follow it. The patient's eyes follow the dancer moving in an elegant, graceful way. The patient becomes absorbed in the oneness, too.

Attention creates the physiological shift that Herbert Benson describes as the relaxation response. The slowing of breathing is typical of meditation and of the relaxation response. The whole physiology changes to parasympathetic arousal, rather than sympathetic arousal.

Reflections on Going through the Veil: Merge with a Greater Power

Let yourself concentrate on great beauty, on sensations of power, on great emotions, on something that takes your interest completely and more deeply than usual. You will be drawn in, taken in without your doing anything except following. Don't worry about the people you are with going, too; this is about you going alone. If the person you are with does not see it, and you do, go farther, not back with that person.

Come in, let yourself go across the veil, follow the voices. Your inner voice appears, a greater voice than yours appears, you have thoughts of reassurance and instruction. Do not be concerned with time. The process of slipping through the veil is timeless. It does not matter how long you stay; it can take only a moment to change your life.

Slipping through the veil is about merging with a greater

power that gives you the assurance you can handle what is happening to you. Let yourself merge with whatever you see and feel. Be completely one with your magnolia. Go into its colors, textures; swim in it; let its odor go into your own cells. Live on the other side of the veil, be there. Move across the veil with consciousness. It has dimension like the surface of water. Oneness with a greater power, connectedness with other people's energies—all are signs of slipping through.

Let yourself concentrate on whatever takes you across the veil. If it is singing, go into the sound fully, until it takes you into energy, and you merge with the sound and are one with it. Take your experience back to life, be it. Take your story to others, make art about it, share it, take possession of it, embody it.

Use Guided Imagery

USING YOUR MIND'S EYE
TO SLIP INTO AND THROUGH THE VEIL

Make yourself comfortable, uncross your legs and arms, close your eyes. Let your breathing slow down, take several deep breaths. Let your abdomen rise as you breathe in and fall as you let your deep breath out. As you breathe in and out, you may feel tingling, buzzing, or relaxation. Allow those feelings to increase. You may feel heavy or light, you may feel your boundaries loosening and your edges soften.

Now let yourself relax. Let your feet relax, let your legs relax. Let the feelings of relaxation spread to your thighs and pelvis. Let your pelvis open and relax. Now let your abdomen relax, let your belly expand; do not hold it in any more. Now let your chest relax, let your heartbeat and breathing take place by themselves. Let your arms relax, your hands relax. Now let your neck relax, your head, your face. Let your eyes relax; see a horizon and blackness for a moment. Let these feelings of relaxation spread throughout your body. Let your relaxation deepen. If you wish, you can count your breaths and let your relaxation deepen with each breath.

Now see yourself in a place you love. It can be in your home, in nature, or in a place in your imagination. Sit down and rest. You can sit on a chair, on the ground, on a magical carpet. Now let yourself drift. Imagine that in front of you, all around you, is a veil. It is a beautiful veil, like a curtain. Or it can look like the surface of the water, a magical membrane that shimmers in the light. Let yourself move toward this veil of light.

Imagine yourself drifting forward or backward, and slowly move toward the shimmering light. Now let yourself pop in one side of the veil. Go into it, like going into a cell. The veil has thickness. You are now inside of it. It is a special place outside of time and space, a magical place that has no equivalent on Earth. Rest there. It is timeless there. You can stay as long as you wish, for there is no time within the magical veil.

Now, when you are ready, drift out the other side of the veil. Let yourself move, like the wind is carrying you. You do not have to do anything, just drift.

Now you are on the other side of the veil. Here everything is different. Here there is no time and space, here it is enchanted, here you are deeply in peace. Here, beauty is everywhere, and you can merge with this beauty whenever you wish.

Look around you. Inside the veil is different for each person. What does your inside of the veil look like? Are there flowers, gardens, waterfalls? Do you see people you love, teachers, deities, animal spirits? Let yourself merge with whatever you see. Be it, feel it, take in its energy. Know that inside the veil is a special place where you can heal, where you can take on the healing energy of whatever is around you.

Let your vision speak to you. If it is a flower, let it call you and invite you in. If it is an animal or a person, let it speak to you and tell you how it will heal you.

Now come back through the veil from the other side. When you are ready, return to the room where you are doing the exercise. First move your feet and then move your hands. Move them around and experience the feeling of the movement. Press your feet down onto the floor, feel the grounding, feel the pressure on the bottom of your feet, feel the solidity of the Earth. Feel your backside on the chair; feel your weight pressing downward. Now open your eyes. Look around you. Stand up and stretch, move your body, feel it move. Come back to your life, see it with new eyes. See the incredible beauty that surrounds you, see the colors, hear the sounds, feel the love. Tell someone you love about your journey, or write it down in a journal. It is yours—the enchantment of the other side of the veil is there for you always.

Chapter 8

✸

Step Five: Know the Truth and Trust the Process

Touched by an Angel

Christopher told us, "I have just heard the news that my cancer has spread to my liver. I am afraid, and I do not want to die. I don't have much energy now. I have lost weight." Tears came to his eyes. He was a tall, elegant man, full of life, and yet now fragile. "I do not want my wife to live without me, to be hurt by all of this. I am separated from my connections to everything around me. I am in the darkness."

We told Chris to tell us about his family. He closed his eyes. He saw his family and told us about his wife, his children. Then he told us about something that he sensed over his shoulder as he looked at his family. He did not see it, he felt it as a presence. We asked him to think about it, to dream and see whether he could see it. The next day, he told us, "An angel is over my shoulder. She calls to me. She is so beautiful." He described her in such detail that we asked him if he knew her. He left and walked in the forest for hours. The next day, he told us, "She is my daughter, she died last year in an accident.

She tells me that she has come back to me to help me heal my cancer. She touches my liver with her fingers, and light comes out of them and goes into me. She is an angel whose heavenly light is healing." He was now at peace. Each day, he would be with her, he would walk through the forest and feel his connection to the Earth, feel the energy of the Earth healing him. His wife called us to wish us merry Christmas. She told us that his cancer had disappeared. The metastatic nodules in his liver were gone.

Know It's the Truth

Knowing the truth was a wonderful experience for all the people in the Spirit Body Healing research study. People described knowing the truth as coming home. The feelings of acceptance turn into self-knowledge. You become a witness of your own life. You know you are on the right path for yourself, and you exist for the greater good of others. You create a place where you have faith in the truth of your life and spiritual dimensions because of your own experience of being embraced by love. You know it is the truth. Every moment is precious and present. Every moment is being in the spiritual dimension.

Knowing the truth is an experience, not a theory. It is a powerful feeling of correctness, of being at home at last, of understanding what has been puzzling you. Knowing the truth is a feeling of certainty, of well-being, of harmony with the universe. Knowing the truth about who you are and what you are to do helps you make decisions in your life, which are in harmony. Knowing the truth is also about knowing you can be healed.

For many participants, knowing the truth was knowing for the first time that they could get better from cancer, arthritis, or depression.

Spirit Body Healing Flows Like a River

In this step, people describe how the process of Spirit Body Healing feels. They often said it was similar to moving like a river. They would "keep flowing." Then, as they saw themselves moving and flowing, they would see themselves change. People describe this process as "being with the next breath." People told us that it is about being present and allowing the process to define them. Surrendering involved releasing the critic, letting go of criticism or judgment or self-condemnation. In surrender, people allow their fear and inadequacies to be there. They accept emotions, the hurt, pain, despair, and rage. They allow these emotions to be there. Surrender also involves finding the way to express the feelings. It includes allowing the storms and hurricanes to be, accepting the velocity of energy that gets released in life. Surrender is about accepting our own darkness, accepting ourselves as a conduit for our emotions to pass through.

Surrender is also about focus, about focusing on our emotions. It is about making a decision to bring intention to the focusing. Surrender involves concentrating on despair, embodying the pain, becoming one with it, merging with it.

Insights of Truth Come Spontaneously

William talks about knowing the truth. He told us he had never done art before, and one day in the hospital, he drew an island surrounded by water, and in the foreground was land and a bridge. He said this drawing was his turning point. When he drew it, he suddenly realized he could now see and find the bridge across the water to the island. In that realization, he felt an insight that he suddenly trusted, and he felt he would get well. In one moment, he knew the truth. He saw and believed completely that he could get well.

His drawings continued to develop, and he drew passionately every day. He shared the images with the staff; he hung them on the walls of his room. He showed them to nurses and doctors. He became excited and encouraged. His art portrayed the journey he was on.

He told me about an experience of walking in a forest:

> I realized I was dealing with the fear of my own death. I was afraid. When I made it through, I realized suddenly what I was afraid of. It was the unknown behind each tree. Then I realized I had nothing to be afraid of. What was behind each tree did not matter. I was not afraid anymore. You know, if you walk down a path in the forest, the smells change as you walk. Did you know the leaves sparkle and become illuminated at their edges, and the shadows dance across the branches? Did you know you can feel the wind shift directions over your body, you can hear each branch rustle, each acorn fall? All of a sudden, I realized I could see out of the eyes of my spirit. I could see the forest illuminated, alive and glimmering in a way. I had never seen it before until I started drawing. That experience was a heightened sense of being, a way of being able to experience life as who I was.

Underneath the Pain Is Always Love

Beth Ames Swartz is an artist pioneer in art and healing. Her piece *Moving Point of Balance* was one of the first large installations of art and healing, and her organization International Transformative Arts was one of the first organizations of its kind. She tells this story of knowing she will get well and trusting the process:

> I felt that underneath the pain was always the love, underneath the fear was always the love. If I could get to the love, I would be all right. When I would carry around the anger

and the rage in my emotions and vicissitudes, I realized that what had happened is my self-esteem had been burnt away in my childhood—literally—and I had to build it painting by painting, piece by piece, series by series.

It is like a new language I have learned through this process. Art again became the residue in the chronicle of what I experienced. The interesting thing is that that pain and fear of the illness wasn't in the paintings. The paintings are beyond that. So I realized that my work is always ahead of my life. And it gave me trust that I will be well.

Truth Comes as a Revelation

Cecelia, a woman with breast cancer, tells us about a revelation of the truth she experienced in a woman's workshop:

> I took a workshop in Santa Fe, New Mexico, a few years ago, and we made prayer sticks. First of all, we did a meditation about what it was that we were to make a prayer stick about. So that was kind of a formal ritual. We got in touch with the first thing that came to our minds, that was what the prayer was to be. Then we went out into the desert, and when we found a stick that really spoke to us, we were to ask the Earth if we could have this stick. Then we were to give something back in return.
>
> We found the stick and then we made the great celebration about preparing the stick for its adornment. You could carve it, you could whittle it, you could make a point at one end. That was amazing, how calming that was; sitting with your little pocket knife and doing this little repetitious carving. Then we all came together, and we brought yarn and feathers and things to the class, and everybody just shared all of these things and just kind of did it again.
>
> We looked at these things, not with the thought that these colors were going to go pretty together, but how these

really affected you. We started off by repeating whatever your prayer was. Then you would start at the top, and you had this elaborate way of wrapping the stick so it would not unravel. Each time you wrapped the stick, you would repeat your prayer. There was this ritual beginning, and at the end, we tied it off so that it would be finished. Then you could embellish it with feathers at the top, so I spent a long time.

When it came my turn to speak to the group about my piece, there was this incredible revelation. It was that this yarn that I had chosen was very frazzled and had all this stuff sticking out from it. The stick I had chosen had a lot of holes in it—it was a choya stick. I suddenly knew that I really had all these holes in myself and I was completely frazzled and I was not together. It just came to me just like that—that was what this stick was all about. That was the beginning of my journey to heal.

The First Insight

You have an insight that suddenly speaks to you. This happened to Mary in her healing with art: "I was looking through books. I found a photo of a woman sitting, and I took it and painted it. The painting was of a woman who had became distorted, messy, she was crying. She was my pain and suffering externalized as art. Form held the emotional experience. I was shocked when I stepped back. I was shocked at who I was. The painting reflected back at me like it was a mirror."

You realize you can go there to find the person who is authentically who you are, and it happens naturally just by doing it.

Reflections on Knowing the Truth and Trusting the Process

Knowing the truth is the age-old experience of understanding that comes with spiritual faith and belief. It is an experience, not a theory; it is based on a surety of feeling. You can recognize knowing the truth because of your feelings of understanding of the universe. Your worldview is all changed now, you understand, it is all clear to you.

There is an experience of all the pieces fitting, of it all being as it should be. It is a belief system coming together. In knowing the truth, you are known, you have a faith based on deep experience and understanding.

Knowing you can get better is a belief you can cultivate. Affirmations, talking to people who have been healed with your condition, talking to a physician or healer who tells you that you can and will get well—all help you believe you will get better.

Dance on One Foot

You can cultivate a belief that you will be cured even if physicians tell you your condition is not curable. We use the metaphor of dancing on one foot to explain our method to patients. We tell them, "For us, belief in being cured is like a dance on one foot. You pick up one foot and put the other down, you then raise that one, and put the one that was up down. In this shamanic dance, you are always standing on one foot with one up."

When you are on your right foot, you hold the thought that the doctor said your condition was likely to recur. When you are on the left foot, you hold the thought that a miracle will heal you, know it will. In this dance of life, you have a choice which foot you stand on. When you stand on one foot, you are on it completely, the other is up. When you are on the foot of the miracle, you believe fully that you will be healed. It is not as if you don't register the information you have been given, but you can also hold a belief that other realities are possible. You can hold two opposite realities at once by dancing on one foot.

In knowing the truth, you will hear an inner voice telling you that your whole belief structure is correct. All of a sudden, insight or knowledge appears to you, and you have knowledge you did not have before.

Find Meaning in Your Own Life

Knowing the truth is also about looking at your life as a story that you believe in intensely. It is about finding meaning and truth in your own life story.

That does not mean all your problems are over or that the illness is cured. It is feeling that what you are doing is the right thing for you to be doing to heal. Knowing the truth often involves a new knowing that you will get well. There is a sudden insight that healing is possible and will happen. Suddenly you know that no matter what a doctor has said or no matter what you have felt, healing is already happening and will continue to happen. To know the truth, it is helpful to frame your life as your own story and to listen to what emerges.

Go with the Flow

Trust in the whole process is going with the flow, letting it happen with the faith that you have from knowing the truth. It takes surrender—you let go into a force that is larger than you are. It takes trust in the stories of others, in your intuition, and in the experiences you are having. Trust strengthens when you have continued experiences of energy, compassion, and transcendence. As you see more and more, your trust deepens. Trust is a process with time. Over time, there are still moments of doubt, but as your experiences become clearer, you can deal with the doubt by understanding it.

Let Go of Negativity

To trust, you must deal with the inner critic who asks, Is this true, or How can you believe in that? You must let the voice of negativity and dissension go and come back to the voice of experience. All of us have doubts in spiritual beliefs—doubt is one of the ways any spiritual process strengthens. With doubt, you analyze what is happening and look closely at who you are and at your feelings and experiences. Then, if you still know the truth and hear the voices of reassurance and support, your faith is increased.

Use Guided Imagery

USING YOUR MIND'S EYE
TO FLOW DOWN YOUR MAGICAL RIVER

Make yourself comfortable, uncross your legs and arms. Close your eyes. Let your breathing slow down, take several deep breaths. Let your abdomen rise as you breathe in and fall as you let your deep breath out. As you breathe in and out, you may feel tingling, buzzing, or relaxation. Let those feelings increase. You may feel heavy or light, you may feel your boundaries loosening and your edges soften.

Now let yourself relax. Let your feet relax, let your legs relax. Let the feelings of relaxation spread to your thighs and pelvis. Let your pelvis open and relax. Now let your abdomen relax, let your belly expand; do not hold it in any more. Now let your chest relax, let your heartbeat and breathing take place by themselves. Let your arms relax, your hands relax. Now let your neck relax, your head, your face. Let your eyes relax; see a horizon and blackness for a moment. Let these feelings of relaxation spread throughout your body. Let your relaxation deepen. If you wish, you can count your breaths and let your relaxation deepen with each breath.

Now see yourself flowing down a magical river. Imagine you are on a large safe raft that carries you like the hand of God. Feel the flow of the water around you, carrying the raft. Feel the current taking you downstream, spinning the raft softly with the bends in the river.

See the water. It is crystal clear, it flows from a sacred spring in the center of God's heart. It is the flow of the universe, the flow to see God. Flow on this perfect current toward the vision of white light that will make you free. Flow on the vision that will show you the face of God.

Feel how it is to be flowing on God's waters downstream, not having to do anything. You are in exactly the right place, where you should be to grow. Everything around is teaching you exactly what you need. You are being taken care of perfectly by the force of universal love.

Know that each thing you see on this flowing is to teach you, to make you grow. Know that each sound of each animal, each bird, is a message to heal. Know that everything that you have done in your life has been done to teach you and make you grow and heal.

Now listen to the voice of the waters, listen as it gurgles and bubbles up from the sacred springs that make the river of God. Listen to what the voice is telling you: "You are perfect. Your voice is clear. You are exactly where you need to be to heal. I love you, you are my baby, you will be healed and give love to everyone you know."

When you are ready, return to the room where you are doing the exercise. First move your feet and then move your hands. Move them around and experience the feeling of the movement. Press your feet down onto the floor, feel the grounding, feel the pressure on the bottom of your feet, feel the solidity of the Earth. Feel your backside on the chair; feel your weight pressing downward. Now open your eyes. Look around you. Stand up and stretch, move your body, feel it move. You are back, you can carry the experience of the exercise outward to your life. You will feel stronger and be able to see deeper. You will be in a healing state. Each time you do the exercise you will be more relaxed and be able to go deeper and more deeply healed.

USING YOUR MIND'S EYE
TO RESTORY YOUR PAST

In your mind's eye, picture an event that was difficult for you. It can be related to your illness, a death of someone you love, a dark time. Now we will see it differently. See a helper, a guide, a spiritual force, someone you love come to you in that event and tell you that she or he loves you. Let the person speak to you, hold you, protect you. See this intensely, deeply as real.

Now rewrite the story of the painful event with the protector and guide as part of it. After all, you are here; something saved you. The spiritual event could have happened—why not use it to take the pain from your past and make your life beautiful?

USING YOUR MIND'S EYE
TO HEIGHTEN YOUR SENSE OF AWARENESS

In your mind's eye, walk down a path in a forest. Feel the soft forest floor under your feet. Hear how it echoes as your footsteps move across it. See how the smells change as you walk, see the leaves sparkle and become illuminated at the edges. See the shadows dance across the branches of each tree. Feel the wind shift directions on your body. Listen to the rustle of branches rubbing against each other. Hear the acorn fall. You see through the eyes of an artist. The forest is illuminated and shimmering in a way you have never seen it before. You feel a heightened sense of being and a heightened sense of seeing your body vibrate.

Chapter 9

✸

Step Six: Embody Your Spirit

The Woman Who Became Pure Love

This is the story of the remarkable death of Michael's wife Nancy, who died of breast cancer in 1993. Many of the people who attended her saw her embody pure spirit. Michael tells us her story:

> Nancy was dying. Her oncologist, whom she loved, had softly told us that she would not live more than a week. She was in a fluctuating coma from liver metastases from her breast cancer. She had fought a courageous battle, and now she was nearing the end of her rich life. As she slipped into her coma, she would have periods when she would be awake and other times when she would drift off to sleep. When she was awake, she took no pain medication, her mind was clear, and she knew what was happening around her.
>
> Five days before her death, she went to a local nursery and bought rose bushes for her English garden. She came home and went upstairs to her bed in the loft of the house she helped build with her own hands. The room had a sky-

light across the entire top of the roof, which was oriented on an ellipsis, and through it, she could see the full moon rise after dark and travel across the skylight and then set before dawn. She could see the stars move from one area of the skylight to another as the Earth rotated and carried her through the night. She could see the mountains across the valley and the city in the distance, where her children had gone to school. She could see the orchard she had pruned and taken care of so lovingly for twenty years.

She climbed upstairs herself that last time, up the steep ladder—like a staircase—barely able to balance. It took all her energy. We supported her and guided her as she climbed upward. She went to the bed where we had slept and made love during most of our marriage, and where she conceived both our children. She sat herself down on the bed and put two pillows behind her head to keep her upright. She did not move from her bed again.

I watched her close her eyes and go into one of her periods of coma. I wondered what her dreams were like, what she was seeing. I was stunned by what was happening, astonished by how brave she was. She awakened clear as a bell and looked around her. I could see immediately that she was different. She looked deep into me. She looked past my personality into my spirit directly. She was like a crystal, almost transparent. I felt something greater than her looking through her into me.

She was also more deeply herself than she had ever been. She told me to ask her closest friends to visit. She said that they could come briefly. The first ones arrived. It was her radiation oncologist and his wife, parents of our older son's best friend. She looked at them, into their eyes, through their bodies into their souls and said, "I love you so much, you are so beautiful." Nothing more. She did not say goodbye. They could not hold back tears. I couldn't either. Our architect and closest friend came. She said, "You are so

STEP SIX: EMBODY YOUR SPIRIT

handsome. I love you so much." Her best friend Elizabeth came and she said, "Elizabeth, I love you so much."

Elizabeth walked downstairs with me. We talked as one friend after another went upstairs, and Nancy told them how beautiful they were and how much she loved them. Elizabeth said, "Michael, do you see that Nancy has become pure spirit? She has shed her personality, and now she is pure light and love." I knew it was true. I had felt it all day. I missed her personality already, but this was magnificent.

Our friend Rachel Remen, a physician Nancy had worked with at a Commonweal cancer retreat and the author of *Kitchen Table Wisdom*, came. She read Nancy a soft story from the bible, about being a mother. Rachel came downstairs and told me, "Nancy is sitting in a Buddhist meditation called Darshan, where she gives the gift of love to each supplicant who comes to her. This is a deep and spiritual gift from one who is on the other side. Michael, this is very beautiful and precious."

Nancy asked for an Episcopalian minister to come, so she could plan her memorial service. I could hear them upstairs laughing. She was telling him stories of her last trip to the English gardens, which she had taken only weeks before. In between stories, she softly pointed out to him the passages she wanted read. She took such care of him and his spiritual task.

Her material work on Earth was done. Now she could drift in and out without speech. Our younger son Lewis played the guitar softly. He played a piece he had written over the previous five days as his mother drifted away. It carried her on her journey to the spirit world. Our older son dug a huge koi pond in the back yard, a ceremonial grave and a deep touching of the Earth that bore him.

The light in the room was now changed. You could see the molecules of air lit up. A visible energy surrounded her and filled the whole room. It was as if the light itself danced around her. The light radiated from itself, and the whole room was lit from within. My oldest friend and medical-school roommate came. The group who would be with her as she died was complete. She could go now.

Elizabeth read a psalm to Nancy as her breathing slowed and finally stopped. I held her hand and watched the light spiral upward like her last breath and leave the room. Our older son went downstairs and cut two roses from her old rose garden. He put the roses on her breasts, sunken and scarred from all her surgeries, and the roses wilted and dried immediately. The green glass candle sticks she had from when she was a little girl cracked with a sound like a lightning bolt downstairs.

Her body lay untouched for three days, as she had asked. On the second night, I had a big dream. I dreamt that I awoke at night. Nancy was next to me in bed alive. I said, "My love, I am so glad you are alive," and I kissed her. She ignored me and stood up and walked to the edge of the loft. There, one of her friends was dressed in white, and her friend awaited her and took her downstairs. The downstairs of our house was filled with grazing goats. Two soft beautiful Latino men had driven up the front lawn in a low-rider car. She walked out the open front door to them. They held out their hands and said, "We are here for you, we have come far." She went to them. The car spiraled up in the sky on a wisp of mist. A face appeared on the mist. It was her, saying good-bye to me. She left, leaving part of her life for me and our boys and taking her spirit to the next place, where she would live in pure love. As she left, she said to me, "Take the pure love I have given you as my spirit." She held out her hands in the vision as if she were giving me the love physically. I saw a dove in her hand, and it flew into mine. She said, "Take this love, and give it to someone, in full, give it all. Give the perfect love from my spirit to her, forever."

Nancy gave me and our boys a wonderful gift through her

embodiment of spirit around her death. I do not know whether she did it on purpose or whether it was a gift from above. It made my grieving for her totally different. I think it made it easier for our boys, too, although losing a mother is different from losing a wife. Nancy's embodiment of spirit was visible to many people. Almost everyone who saw her and received Darshan from her noticed it and commented on it. It is not hard to see, but it is hard to accept. We are not taught to look for the embodiment of spirit in ordinary people around us, even when they are about to leave.

You Can Embody Spirit

Near death, people often embody pure spirit. The embodiment of spirit is incredibly beautiful and moving to everyone who sees it. Holy people like the pope and the Dalai Lama are a living embodiment of spirit. You can feel it when they come near you. People come to see them from afar. You can feel their energy, see the light around them, feel their effect on everyone. You can understand in the center of your being how they are the embodiment of pure spirit. Seeing them is believed to be a great blessing. Having them touch you is believed to be healing. Christ was the embodiment of pure spirit, as were the holy people of all religions.

From our research study, we believe that it is possible for ordinary people to embody spirit, too. Each of us has the capability to become spirit, to radiate light and love, to give ourselves as a sacred gift, as Darshan, to anyone who comes to visit us to receive us as the ultimate gift. In the stories of our participants, we often saw the embodiment of spirit. Sometimes the people themselves were aware of it, and those around them were, too; sometimes they were not. As you read the stories in this book, you can feel the embodiment of spirit yourself. As you read the stories, you can see the air change, the light change, the energy change completely. You can feel the person acting from a part of them that is far deeper than their personality.

When people embody pure spirit, they are beautiful. Like Nancy, they radiate light, they send their love to you without ego or expectation of anything in return. They are pure love.

I Was Just Wondering: A Story of Grace

Kareem, a beautiful ten-year-old boy, is receiving a bone-marrow transplant for leukemia. He is on his third bone-marrow transplant. He is reacting to the medication, and his skin is falling off. The nurses have bandaged his hands softly so that he can still move. His family has finally accepted the fact that he is dying.

He looks at the bandages on his hands and asks the nurse, "I was wondering if you could take these bandages off my hands." The nurse says she cannot. He says, "Oh, I was just wondering, thank you." He is as soft as the morning dew, as light as the gentlest breeze at dawn. In the morning peace, he is dying. He is totally filled with grace; there is incomprehensible gentleness in the room. He is pure innocence and pure power at once. At the threshold, he is filled with incredible light and beauty.

She Became Part of the Spirit of the Earth

Julia was extremely depressed because a relationship had ended. The woman who had left her had been cruel to her. Julia told us that she felt abused, almost run over. She felt worthless. The woman had told Julia that Julia was evil, a witch. Julia was confused and really could not function. She had left her job and was sitting at home crying. She had seen several physicians and healers. She had been taking antidepressants, and they stopped her crying but were dulling her perceptions, and she felt little better.

She tried everything she could think of to get better. She

went for long walks, gardened, and did guided imagery. It was helping. The time alone to go into her dreams and herself was giving her solace. On her daily walks, she would do the same imagery. She would picture herself in the forest she was walking in, she would picture herself part of the world she walked through. She did not know where that idea came from, but it became part of her walk. As the days went by, in her imagery, she saw herself growing. She did not know what this meant, but she had a constant image of herself as a plant in the forest. In her image, she was green, she had leaves as her skin, she had vines and stems as her bones, strong roots as her feet.

One evening, she went to a lecture by an artist who showed her slides of painting the bellies of pregnant woman. The artist said she did that to help the women see themselves as beautiful. Julia decided to have several friends who were painters paint her body. She tells us her story:

> We went up to the studio of one of my friends. It was above the city, high in the air. It had skylights that reached towards the sun. The beautiful sunlight filled the room with brightness. I knew it was the right place. I took my clothes off, and we got out the paints. I stood in the center of the huge room. My friends had never done this before; they were both happy and dubious about it. They asked me what I wanted painted on my body. I told them that I had seen myself as a plant, and just then, I saw a beautiful painting my friend had made of a climbing vine with open flowers on it.
>
> They started on my belly and painted a spiral place of great beauty. It was the Earth, it had a seed which was sprouting. They were enjoying it. They told me that when they painted something that was right for me, they could feel it in their bodies, they knew.
>
> I closed my eyes and rested. I could not see what they were painting. I felt the brushes on my belly, arms, and legs. I felt like I was being cared for, caressed by the Earth.

I opened my eyes and looked in the full-length mirror that was on the wall behind us. I gasped. My friends all told me I looked beautiful. I looked at my body, and I was proud of it and felt secure. I was beautiful. My body had turned into a lush tropical vine with opening purple and orange flowers. The vine came from the pod on my uterus and went everywhere. My friends laughed. I closed my eyes again. They continued painting.

I felt this enormous energy of the Earth coming up into me. I felt the sunlight coming into my body. I felt the wind from the open windows. I felt the water from the paints cool on my body. My body was electric. It pulsed and sent out waves of energy. As I breathed, my cells lit up, and I could feel the air and sunlight coming into each cell. I loved this. It felt so good. I felt like I was connected deeply to my friends and to the Earth.

Now the woman who had hurt me was gone. During the ritual, she had left, been driven off. My friends had replaced her with their love and beauty. The whole Earth was my lover now. I was cared for, connected, and purified. My hurt was over. She was gone. All of her abuse was now not relevant to my life. I was growing by myself. I had become the green colors and flowers in the living Earth.

Allow Spirit to Come into You from the Earth

Somewhere in the process, participants move to a place of embodying spirit. Again, it is a spiral. The embodiment of spirit might take place in the first thing a person does after being in the darkness, or only after years. In the creative process, the participants explored the embodiment of spirit and Spirit Body Healing. The stories reveal an experience that is moving and like a spiritual teaching.

You Are a Person of Spirit and Power

Embodying the spirit makes people look at their lives from a new perspective. They look at each event in a new way. Events that did not happen before happen now. They see a beacon of hope where there was only breast cancer, they see themselves as an open woman where there was only fear and pain. They restory the events of the past, and they can restory their whole lives. They change the past in the present.

She Embodied Spirit and Prayer

James sits with his wife in a bone-marrow transplant unit. She has leukemia and is very ill. She has had the chemotherapy drugs that will kill all growing cells in her body and has had bone marrow put back into her so her blood can keep her alive. The powerful chemotherapy has left her in pain and without energy. James tells the story:

> I woke up each day and saw her suffering. I could see that the sores from the cells that had been killed in her mouth were extremely painful for her. She took morphine to even be able to swallow. I hurt me deeply to see and feel her pain. I decided to write down what was happening. It was the first time I had ever tried to journal. The first day I started to write, I started to complain about how bad this all was. I started to list the things that were going wrong.
>
> And the most surprising thing happened. I looked at my wife and started to describe her. I was planning on writing how bad she looked, how she was bald from hair loss, and how her skin was pale. Instead I saw her as beautiful.
>
> It was dawn. The sun was just rising. Her room had wonderful windows facing east. The newborn sun hit her face and lit her up. She was still asleep. My eyes opened. It was as

if light came from her to meet the morning sun. It was as if her light was as bright as the light of the sunrise.

And then a prayer came to me. I wrote, "Thank you for this day. Thank you for my wife and her beauty. Thank you for her doctors and nurses and for the care she is receiving that will save her life. Please help her, she is a good woman. Do what is right for her now in our lives. If it is your will, help make her well."

I was shocked. I had never prayed before, and I had certainly never prayed for anyone to get well. Yet it just came to me as I started to write in my journal. From that day, I wrote each morning at sunrise. And each morning, my complaints and fears turned to seeing beauty and to a prayer of thanks and a prayer for her healing.

As people do things to heal, whether it is walking or gardening, the spirit comes into them, and they are profoundly changed. This man's simple journaling took him from fear to prayer. By letting something emerge from deep inside of him, which he did not control, he was new. With many of our participants, prayer came to them naturally when they embodied spirit. As the spirit entered them, they found themselves praying in thanks, in reverence, and in supplication. In the story of Nancy that started this chapter, her best friend Elizabeth recited the psalm as Nancy died. This was natural, unplanned. It came into the room as Nancy's spirit left.

Reflections on the Embodiment of Spirit

The embodiment of spirit is beyond personality—it is letting the greater power within you emerge. Yet, paradoxically, you are yourself more purely than you have ever been. You are love, you are light, you are a gift given from beyond the Earth.

Be the Love That You Are

To let yourself embody spirit, let your personality go and be who you are—be the love and light that you feel, without the things that make you afraid to let it out. You can do this without words. It is beyond your work, your family, the things you are good at. It is pure and without form; it is you as a crystal, without the body.

You can do this. The teaching of the stories is that anyone can. It takes letting go and letting something deep and beautiful enter us. It is a letting go of fear, of holding back, of conditioning. In our research, it was most obvious near death, but we saw it in the most ordinary moments with the most ordinary people.

Expect Nothing in Return

It can be seen. The light and energy around the person changes, miracles appear. Is the embodiment of spirit a gift? It is easier to see and maybe even to do than to accept. You can feel the energy and see the light. Let go of your ego, expect nothing in return for your love. Be pure love, and do not expect your family or friends to do anything. Let go of pain of rejection and neediness. Accept your own deepest gentleness, softness, grace, and innocence, and you will find your greatest power.

It sounds difficult if not impossible to embody spirit, but when you have slipped through the veil, seen an angel, felt healing energy, it can be done. We are all pure spirit, and to let it be seen, all we need to do is step out of the way.

Use Guided Imagery

USING YOUR MIND'S EYE
TO BECOME PURE LOVE

Make yourself comfortable, uncross your legs and arms, close your eyes. Let your breathing slow down, take several deep breaths, let your abdomen rise as you breathe in and fall as you let your deep breath out. As you breathe in and out, you may feel tingling, buzzing, or relaxation. Let those feelings increase. You may feel heavy or light, you may feel your boundaries loosening and your edges soften.

Now let yourself relax. Let your feet relax, let your legs relax. Let the feelings of relaxation spread to your thighs and pelvis. Let your pelvis open and relax. Now let your abdomen relax, let your belly expand; do not hold it in any more. Now let your chest relax, let your heartbeat and breathing take place by themselves. Let your arms relax, your hands relax. Now let your neck relax, your head, your face. Let your eyes relax; see a horizon and blackness for a moment, let these feelings of relaxation spread throughout your body. Let your relaxation deepen. If you wish, you can count your breaths and let your relaxation deepen with each breath.

Now you will embody spirit. This is easier to do than you would imagine—it is simply a letting go. First, let your personality drift away. Let your name, where you live, your job, and your family drift off. If you are not comfortable with this, just let something you do drift away—driving a car, cooking dinner—let something that you identify with fall off, and just be who you are without it.

Now see yourself as the light within you, without your specific characteristics that make you an individual in this lifetime. See the love you have, the generosity, your service, your ability to see visions of spirit. Let these parts of you grow and replace the parts of you that are personality. Let worry, anger, hate, family issues, job problems fall aside and be replaced by love and beauty.

To help you do this, imagine that you are on vacation, that all is taken care of perfectly at home, that each person you take care of, each job concern is covered with perfect care by someone you trust. On this special vacation, you need only be yourself without doing anything at all. You do not have to cook, drive, take care of anyone, do anything.

Now let the feelings of love you feel when you are most in touch with love come up into you and intensify. Let the visions of God, angels, spirit, nature that you have had in your life come to you and merge with you. Let the visions send out a beam of light, and let your spirit go up that beam into their heart and let their love come down to you. You do not need anything in return for giving this love. You need nothing when you are pure love.

Picture that pure love, pure generosity, pure heavenly care is in your heart, that you are one with these feelings. Now imagine that a wonderful light comes from within you from heaven and can be seen by everyone.

Now just rest. Allow the love and light that are your soul to flow out of you and be seen by everyone. There is nothing for you to do. Just let it come from the center of the universe, from its heart into you, and pass out to the world, to all those around you, to the whole Earth.

USING YOUR MIND'S EYE
TO EMBODY YOUR SPIRIT IN A MOMENT

Imagine that you are in a difficult situation. You can be at home with tension and chaos, you can be rushed or overwhelmed, or you can be dealing with problems concerning an illness or other life crisis. Then imagine letting that place go. Picture yourself turning around and dancing as your spirit. See yourself whirl and spin, see yourself expand and fly. Then go into the center of the spinning, and see through the eyes of your spirit, and see your own light. See yourself as radiant, as a source of light and energy. Now come back to your ordinary life and still see yourself as enchanted. Imagine you are above yourself and see yourself as pure beauty.

You are love and pure beauty.

CHAPTER 10

Step Seven: Feel the Healing Energy of Love and Compassion

Feeling Serpent Energy

Linda had been sick for months with ovarian cancer. In addition to her chemotherapy, she had done everything she could think of to get well. She had used meditation and changed her diet. She had gone to many healers. Nonetheless, even with her pain medication and with all she had done, she was still in severe pain. Linda tells us her story:

> I would hurt every day. I would awaken to pain. I thought sometimes I could not stand it. There were moments when it was like I was being stabbed with a knife. Sometimes the pain would come and build, and I would think that I would have to kill myself. The pain could come on suddenly any time, and I would become so afraid I would call anyone I knew and cry and beg for help.
>
> After one horrible episode, I thought more deeply about what I could do. I knew I had to do something. I thought back on my whole life, and I tried to find what I had ever

done that had helped me. I started listing what had helped me. I had been to India and meditated, I had been in women's groups. I looked at each thing I had done in the past to heal myself, and then I closed my eyes and rested to see how that would feel now in my body. I let images come to me and leave, just as I had been taught in meditation.

Then I saw a vision. I saw myself lying in the middle of a fire and floating there. I saw myself surrounded by flames and full of energy and very much alive. I did not know what to do, so I called my friends on the phone and told them about my vision. Then we got this idea: We made a date to all meet at a house near me and do a healing ritual.

My friends came, and each brought candles. One friend brought a small Zuni fetish serpent carved from stone. We went into the living room. Then I got sick and lay on the couch. I was in so much pain that I could not really move. As my friends set up their candles, I went deeper and deeper into a trance. I was in pain, but for some reason, it was not as frightening to me as it usually was. My friends started to make an altar for me with the beautiful things they had brought. They moved slowly like dancers. I had told about my vision of the fire, but they seemed to know more than I knew, and they just started working. It was like an ancient female knowledge took over. They took a beautiful cloth with a mandala pattern of flames in the center of it and put in on the floor. They put a red heart-shaped pad on the cloth, so I could lie down on it and be comfortable. They put the candles they had brought in a circle around the altar they had made. They put offerings of flowers and put little animals all around the cloth.

My closest friend came and got me and escorted me to the center of the ceremonial altar. She took my hand; I felt like a queen or a respected elder. I moved slowly and felt elegant and sacred. She lay me down. I slipped my clothes

STEP SEVEN: FEEL THE HEALING ENERGY OF LOVE AND COMPASSION

away so my belly was visible. My friends covered me with the flowers at first, and then ceremonially brushed them off me. The friend who brought the serpent put it on my body over the scar from my surgery. I closed my eyes. My friends began to sing softly and to chant. I drifted off and came back and drifted off again. I could see my pain, far away, standing alone in the center of a huge expanded space. It started walking away and got smaller and smaller. The space got bigger and bigger. The pain walked further away, and then I could not see it anymore.

Now my friends lit the candles. The fire surrounded me. All I saw were the flames. In my dreamlike state, they seemed to rise higher and come all around my body. Then I went deeper and started dreaming. In my dream, I saw myself floating in the air like I was levitating. Flames were all around me. And then something happened. I felt something come up into my body from below. It tapped on my back and then came into me.

I knew instantly it was my serpent. I call it my serpent even though I had never had a serpent before. The snake came up through the skin on my back and went to where my uterus and ovaries had been before my surgery. It became larger and filled my lower abdomen. It became wider, and I saw spots and saw its colors become brighter. As I saw this serpent, I felt an energy come up into me that shocked and startled me. I started shaking and vibrating. For a moment, I saw myself from above. I was lying on the floor, and I saw my friends holding me as I shook. I felt an enormous buzzing coming from the base of my spine and felt heat rising within me. I stopped shaking, and the heat and vibration rose up to where my uterus has been.

I received a message: "You are giving birth to yourself. Within your magical uterus, you are giving birth to your new self." I could see my uterus was now lit up, on fire. It was outlined in fire, it was electric. I felt the enormous energy of the primordial fire within me. I felt the serpent rise from the base of my spine to my abdomen and then up to my heart and my throat and my head.

I opened my eyes and saw the serpent around my spine larger than my body. I felt the enormous energy of the serpent filling me and coming out of my eyes and out of the top of my head. I looked around me. I felt the fire cleansing me and purifying me. My friends were there. They were now outside the circle, they looked like they were praying. I started crying. They cried, too. I felt no pain. I felt only a calmness and a peace that was more than my understanding.

Weeks later, she was still pain free. She started exercising again, and as she ran, each day, she felt the energy of the serpent and the fire arise within her and go to her legs and carry her forward on her healing journey.

Feel Compassion and Healing Energy

Another major theme that emerged in the Spirit Body Healing study was the experience of feeling healing energy and compassion. In talking about their healing, the participants discussed moving from one perception of reality to another. A typical story told of the participant going from an experience of the illness as only pain to a different experience of the illness as spiritual growth. This transformation was articulated in a number of ways. Some people described it as feelings of deep compassion for themselves. They had sudden feelings of self-love, experiencing a deeper understanding of themselves. Participants told of experiencing a heightened awareness of their bodies in their own lives, a heightened experiencing of the world around them. They felt a huge energy come into them from inside and outside, which they all called healing energy.

STEP SEVEN: FEEL THE HEALING ENERGY OF LOVE AND COMPASSION

Healing Energy Is an Ancient Concept

Healing energy is a central concept in healing. Most healing systems throughout history have had concepts of healing energy that were basic to how people healed. When people talk of healing, when they experience healing, they feel energy. When we talk of a resonance of the body, mind, and spirit, we mean a freeing of energy, a buzzing, a tingling, a vibration, a hovering. The energy is felt as a sensation, a feeling—it can flow throughout the body, from body to body, from the universe to us. It has been seen by psychics and meditators and has been portrayed in art. Perhaps the simplest metaphor for how the spirit heals is that it frees the flow of our bodies' healing energy.

Spinning and Letting Go

In letting go, you go to a place within you. A dancer told this story of letting go:

> When I'm just dancing, riding on music or without music, it's like spiraling. As I dance, the image is like spiraling, even though that's not physically what I'm doing. But as I'm spiraling, the stuff that doesn't need to be there for me flies off. It flings off, as when you're spinning something and the stuff spins off. Everything gets clearer and lighter and cleaner, and I get inside and then, pop, I find that place that is just free.

The Christmas Card Photo

Ree walked down the hall in the intensive care unit. He was in heart failure and kidney failure due to years of alcoholism. He had stopped drinking eight years before and was in a twelve-step program. He was dressed in a hospital gown that barely covered him. His wife walked beside him. He looked awful. He had dropped to ninety pounds from one hundred and fifty. He was yellow, and his skin was literally coming off him due to a drug reaction. A catheter was in his penis, and IV tubes were in his central line, connected to three pumps that were hung on the pole he pushed as he walked. His heart rhythm was off, which was life threatening. Ree told this story:

> As we walked, my gown fell open. You know hospital gowns don't work well; their tie is ridiculous. I stood in the hall, exposed and almost naked. The catheter in my penis hung down, filled with a dark brown fluid, my skin hung off me and fell off me in patches. My face was like death.
>
> I looked at my wife walking beside me. She looked back at me, she looked directly into my eyes. I saw her. Time stopped. The room opened up. The hallway disappeared. We were alone in a space that felt like it was full of energy. I said, "Honey, maybe we should have a picture taken of this and put it on our Christmas card." I laughed, a laughter so large it filled the hallway. My face opened up, and my wife said it seemed to fill with light. She laughed, too. She opened up and laughed and patted me, and we seemed to merge in our laughter.

Then, even though they had been told by all the doctors he would die, he suddenly improved. He said:

> When I saw myself standing in the hallway, I saw how awful I looked. I saw myself dying. It was as if in that moment a part of me rose up in the air and could see me and Betty walking below me and could see my gown open. In that moment, I was up looking and down walking at once. My body felt like it was buzzing. It was also filled with light. It was so

beautiful I forgot where and almost who I was. I was entranced.

Then I remembered what was happening, and I saw myself and Betty walking again. Now we were in this glow. In a peaceful place. Just then, I was myself, and I told the joke to Betty. Now I did not think of it, it just came to me. And when I told it, I was different. I was my old self, powerful, integral, strong. I was not the man in the hospital hallway. For a moment, the joke took me elsewhere to a place where I was alive and joyful. I was not going to die, no way.

We saw Ree sitting by a swimming pool six years after that incident. He had just gotten out of a hospital where he had almost died again. His wife told me he had popped up again like a rubber duck in a tub. His spirit was as large as an angel.

Use Humor to Release Healing Energy

The preceding story is about feeling healing energy, the enormous life-saving positivity of vitality even when a person has a life-threatening illness. It reminds us that there is more to the experience of illness than being sick in this moment.

Black humor allowed them almost to escape from the illness. Every health-care provider has seen this happen. The health-care providers crack the black jokes themselves to survive the pressure. In *The House of God*, a book about a resident in a hospital, black humor is used by staff members to deal with situations like this. In Ree's humor is the release of his laughter. Since the time this story took place, Ree has made videos, telling this story to help other alcoholics deal with illness. He sends jokes by e-mail, writes joke books, and lectures about this story to people who are very ill. He looks at you deeply, and you feel his spirit and its power and you feel you will get better from anything as long as you live.

Feeling the Body Sensations of Healing Energy

Shondra describes healing energy:

> This experience has a very traditional kind of yoga quality. That's what happens when I get going into this state. The quality of light shifts, and everything takes on a kind of humming quality.
>
> My whole vision brightens and, you know, it's very interesting. I had one vision in which I could see that everything is really energy. What we think of as solid—your body, my body, the table, the chairs—is really just molecules of atoms vibrating at different frequencies and densities, and what we see as the illusion of reality is really just all vibration of energy.

This description of seeing energy is common to several of the participants in Mary's study. One woman said she saw the molecules of air as alive; they were moving and full of light. One man saw the lines of space that connect objects and people as electric lines of light.

Being Held and Rocked

Olivia was a frail old woman, and she sat slightly hunched over. She told us that she had breast cancer, and her husband had left her while she was ill. She said that he told her he just could not deal with this, he had other things to do in life. She sat and softly cried. We both wanted to hold her. A part of us reached out for her from somewhere deep within. We held back and continued the interview. She told us the story of her illness, and then we asked her if she had an image of what would be healing to her in this difficult situation. This was her response: "When I was a young girl, I would go the beach. I was so strong. I was beautiful and lithe, my muscles could

STEP SEVEN: FEEL THE HEALING ENERGY OF LOVE AND COMPASSION

move so easily. I would stretch and bend and turn and dance in the morning sun."

As Olivia said this, we could see her as a young girl. We could see her arriving at the beach in Los Angeles in a time when the air was still clear. We could see her in a bathing suit of the era, and we could see her face without wrinkles, in its girlish beauty. We looked at her face now, and we could see it turning into her girlish face as she told us her story. We could see her wrinkles disappearing and her face relaxing to a face she has not had for many years. We could also see her body unwinding, stretching, becoming larger. It was as if she opened up, and her arms and legs lengthened and became young again. Right in front of us, she stretched out as though she was putting her head back into the morning sun.

"I would go down to the beach and sit on the cement steps leading down to the water. I would put my head back in the sun, and the whole world was mine; the Earth itself would hold me and caress me and take care of me. I felt so at home, so much myself."

We asked her what we could do to help her now. She said, "Please hold me and rock me." So we went to her, and she lay in our laps, and we held her so gently and rocked her as the Earth would do. Now we were the Earth, and she was our baby, whom we loved. We looked down at her, from a long distance; we looked directly into her eyes with total love. We saw her as she was in every moment of her life. We saw her as a baby, as a young girl. We saw her as a young mother, a middle-aged woman, and we saw her, too, as a wise old woman. We saw her in her timeless persona, as her spirit. She absorbed it and was her spirit and sent her beauty to us and saw her timeless beauty herself. She hugged each of us and left. When we talked to her months later, she told us she has been in a place of great inner peace. She still felt timeless, and she still felt loved. She was able to carry the feeling with her for months.

Feel Compassion for Yourself

From our research, we learned that spirit healing is also about feeling compassion. It is about feeling compassion for yourself if you are ill and feeling compassion for your patient if you are a healer. The compassion is timeless and not dependent on personality. It is pure and eternal. Pure compassion is a part of all spiritual practice. In Buddhist meditation, you go to a place where there is total compassion. You go to a place where you restory your life from the place of compassion and love.

Our study showed that the restorying was crucial in the healing process. One woman told us, "I became compassionate for myself by seeing myself from a distance, from outside. I looked at her below me. I saw her tears, her sadness. I saw how needy she was. I stood back and said to myself, 'Look at her. I will love her right now as she is.' In a moment of witness, of reflection, I could see what I needed to heal."

Reflections on Healing Energy and Compassion: Release Judgment and See with Compassion

Feel compassion for yourself, along with feelings of healing energy. This part is more difficult to do than simply feeling energy. We are all very judgmental toward ourselves, and it is hard to release the eye of the inner critic.

Restory your view of yourself as someone who can see yourself with compassion, as someone who is compassionate. You can do an exercise to increase your feelings of compassion. Practice seeing out of the eyes of the Buddha, of Mother Teresa, or of the most compassionate person you can think of. Look at yourself through their eyes. That exercise is a practice called the Buddha of Compassion. Let the deity or compassion person you choose gaze at you with compassionate eyes and see yourself completely with love. Let the person see you

STEP SEVEN: FEEL THE HEALING ENERGY OF LOVE AND COMPASSION

inside and outside. Just letting yourself be seen compassionately is enormous.

After you let yourself be seen compassionately by a compassionate one, imagine the compassionate one entering your body and filling you up to the very capacity, the very edges of your skin, and see the world through this person's eyes. See through the eyes of compassion. As you do this, you are yourself, but you're also seeing through the eyes of compassion. If you are a judgmental person, or you have expectations, give yourself over to the one who fills you and gives you the ability to have compassion. When you are present with another person and see that person without judgment, with love and acceptance, what you see is that person's beauty and uniqueness.

The practice of the Buddha of compassion is helpful to increase your ability to feel compassion toward yourself. If your grandmother is the most compassionate person you have ever known, imagine that you are sitting across from your grandmother, and she is looking at you with total love and acceptance. Just sit there and be with her, and allow yourself to be seen, and ask her to help you not be judgmental toward yourself as you heal with spirit.

Use Guided Imagery

USING YOUR MIND'S EYE
TO FEEL HEALING ENERGY

Make yourself comfortable, uncross your legs and arms, close your eyes. Let your breathing slow down, take several deep breaths. Let your abdomen rise as you breathe in and fall as you let your deep breath out. As you breathe in and out, you may feel tingling, buzzing, or relaxation. Let those feelings increase. You may feel heavy or light; you may feel your boundaries loosening and your edges soften.

Now let yourself relax. Let your feet relax, let your legs relax. Let the feelings of relaxation spread to your thighs and pelvis. Let your pelvis open and relax. Now let your abdomen relax, let your belly expand; do not hold it in any more. Now let your chest relax, let your heartbeat and breathing take place by themselves. Let your arms relax, your hands relax. Now let your neck relax, your head, your face. Let your eyes relax; see a horizon and blackness for a moment. Let these feelings of relaxation spread throughout your body. Let your relaxation deepen. If you wish, you can count your breaths and let your relaxation deepen with each breath.

Now, as you breathe, let the feelings of tingling, buzzing, or vibrations increase. Pay attention to where in your body the feelings are the most intense. It may be your fingertips, your hands, your abdomen. Wherever it is, let the feeling grow. With each breath, let your own feelings of healing energy strengthen.

Now see the feelings as colors. Each person will have her or his own color for each area. Let a color appear to you. As you breathe in, the color will get brighter—as you breathe out, impurities will leave, and the color will get clearer.

Now let the energy flow, and begin to move. Let the energy move from where it was first most intense to flow throughout your body. Let it move to the center of your body and up and down your spinal cord. If you wish, you can let it start at the bottom and move upward. If you know about energy centers or chakras, let your own healing energy stop and rest and concentrate in each of your chakras before it moves on. Let your healing energy move from the base of your spine upward to the top of your head and back again in a circular motion.

If you found areas that were blocked, let the energy move around them, through them, jump over them, whatever feels natural to you. Let the energy wash over the blockage and move on.

Now let the energy strengthen. You can let it increase like a heat getting warmer, or you can let it start to move like a vi-

STEP SEVEN: FEEL THE HEALING ENERGY OF LOVE AND COMPASSION

bration or trembling. Let this process happen by itself, let it grow, and if there is an image associated with it, let the image grow.

Now take the enhanced energy and let it wash your whole body clean. Let it move throughout your body and purify, cleanse, and heal you. If you see any areas of grayness, let this immense healing energy wash the density out. You can see the energy increase as you breathe in and the darkness leave as you breathe out.

After you let the energy build and move, just rest. Let the feelings of peace come over you. Let the energy stay where it is now and balance within your body. Let the energy seek a center and then move out from there evenly, where it is needed in the rest of your body.

When you are ready, return to the room where you are doing the exercise. First move your feet and then move your hands. Move them around and experience the feeling of the movement. Press your feet down onto the floor, feel the grounding, feel the pressure on the bottom of your feet, feel the solidity of the Earth. Feel your backside on the chair; feel your weight pressing downward. Now open your eyes. Look around you. Stand up and stretch, move your body, feel it move. You are back, you can carry the experience of the exercise outward to your life. You will feel stronger and be able to see deeper. You will be in a healing state. Each time you do the exercise you will be more relaxed and be able to feel healing energy more deeply.

USING YOUR MIND'S EYE TO EXPERIENCE COMPASSION

Make yourself comfortable. Uncross your legs and arms, close your eyes. Let your breathing slow down, take several deep breaths, let your abdomen rise as you breathe in and fall as you let your deep breath out. As you breathe in and out, you may feel tingling, buzzing, or relaxation. Let those feelings increase. You may feel heavy or light; you may feel your boundaries loosening and your edges soften.

Now let yourself relax. Let your feet relax, let your legs relax. Let the feelings of relaxation spread to your thighs and pelvis. Let your pelvis open and relax. Now let your abdomen relax, let your belly expand; do not hold it in any more. Now let your chest relax, let your heartbeat and breathing take place by themselves. Let your arms relax, your hands relax. Now let your neck relax, your head, your face. Let your eyes relax; see a horizon and blackness for a moment. Let these feelings of relaxation spread throughout your body. Let your relaxation deepen. If you wish, you can count your breaths and let your relaxation deepen with each breath.

Now see yourself sitting in your home in a place that is comfortable. Picture the most compassionate person you can imagine sitting across from you. It can be a person you know—a loved one, a family member, a religious figure, a teacher, a presence from nature. Picture that person looking at you, right into your eyes as deeply as imaginable. Let her or him look right into your soul, past your personality. Let this person see you in your most beautiful aspect, as the most loving person you can be. The one you chose can do this—that is why you have chosen this person to come. Let that feeling of being seen with compassion come over you completely. Absorb the way it feels to be loved without limits, without conditions. Feel the universal love come over you.

Now go into that person's body, and look through her or his eyes. Imagine you can see yourself the way you were just seen. See yourself as endlessly beautiful, as perfectly loving, as the way you are beyond your personality. See yourself the way you are seen by Jesus, by the Great Spirit, by the Buddha, by the Blessed Mother.

You are that person. You can have compassion for yourself the way that person has compassion for you.

Chapter 11

✦

Step Eight: Experience Transcendence

There Is No Death, Only Life Everlasting

Collin had cancer of the colon with metastases to the liver. In partial liver coma, he was sleeping half of the time. He was taking no pain medicine so when he was awake, he was clear. One day he came out of his bedroom to make himself breakfast. His children and his wife were still asleep. Even in his situation he felt a deep sense of peace.

Collin let himself drift into deep thought. He had been sick for years and in the peace of this morning, he now could see that he was constantly carrying a tension about dying with him. It did not have to do with his family, his finances, or his religious beliefs. It was about something deeper. Collin tells us his story:

> I was standing in the kitchen. The silence surrounded me and seemed like a presence that was caring for me. I heard it as a buzzing in my ears, like bees at a great distance. The sun was rising over the mountains across the valley in front of my house. The light was increasing every moment. The

light was opening and expanding. I felt the light in my chest as relaxation. It was as if the light was opening me. It was coming to me from somewhere or someone and, like fingers in a massage, it was opening my heart.

I closed my eyes. I saw more light with my eyes closed than with them open. This was happening more and more to me as I became more ill. I took a deep breath. As I breathed in, the space around me opened. It became darker and the space opened further and further. It seemed like the walls of a huge stadium were being pulled away. And then the light came from beyond them and I was in a place where there were no limits. The quiet was gone; now there was a sense of expectancy. It was a waiting that had a noise to it like a soft rain.

And from within the opening light, from within the soft, even background noise was a presence, a voice, a power. I heard and thought at once, "There is no death, only life everlasting." The presence or information came from within me and outside of me at once. It came again, "There is no death, only life everlasting." It came from everywhere. It seemed to me that it had been there forever. It was speaking directly to me. I knew that it was God speaking. I understood it deeper than my bones. Again it said, "There is no death, only life everlasting."

And as I heard this again, I knew for the first time what it meant. I knew it as a certainty, a powerful depth of understanding that was timeless. I knew in my body, in my cells. I knew that whatever I was and my wife was and my children were was not something that ended or went away. I knew that I was simply here forever and as the sun rose, I saw my death as something as natural as the sun rising across the soft valley behind the mountains of green.

I knew then that my death would not stop me from being who I was in my essence and who I would be, forever. I opened my eyes and my wife was standing next to me. She was looking at me with so much love, crying softly like the rain. I kissed her from where I had been, and I said to her, "My love, there is no death, only life everlasting." And I felt her soft touch and knew I would always feel it and she would always feel mine.

From that moment on, I felt a deep sense of peace and calmness that was new for me. I looked deeply into her eyes, and I cried, too. It was very sad what was happening to us, but I knew, I had been told, it was all right.

He died several months later. His death was so peaceful, it seemed as if it really was part of nature, as soft as the gentle rain. He did not seem to have any fear, he was full of love. When we visited him the day before he died, he kissed us and thanked us for listening to his story and for taking care of him. We looked at him a long time. We cried to be losing this patient and dear friend. And we learned far more from him than he learned from us.

See Yourself As Surrounded by God and the Angels

The final theme in Spirit Body Healing, transcendence, concerns the experience of feelings of oneness. Each participant in our research study described feeling profound experiences of transcendence, of an immense interconnectedness. These feelings were like the ones they felt initially in slipping through the veil, but now they were deeper and more fully formed.

Glimpses of God or angels that they had in the beginning of their healing journey grew immensely in their power and meaning. Participants experienced the power of the universe, felt the presence of God, and often heard the voice of God. They felt they had emerged in another dimension, one of great power and beauty. Transcendence was like hearing a message from God. Because messages from God are often associated with being overzealous, participants in our study were reluctant to share the experiences with us initially. It required trust for them to tell us these stories fully. They had to believe we would honor them and listen with an open mind.

Share Your Love

People also felt they were vehicles to share love and communicate love. People would report seeing themselves for the first time, discovering within themselves a place of ecstasy. One woman told us, "I spent years trying to find myself. I did it all. I did body work, meditation, rolfing, women's groups. Then I got really sick, and I went inside myself and painted. Then I found myself and she was right smack inside. It's the biggest joke in the world. You go out in the world to find yourself, and you find her inside—who would have thought?"

Illuminosity: Be within the Light

After you go inward, glimpse darkness and light, feel or see your spirit, and feel healing energy, you experience luminosity.

For most study participants, their body feelings of luminosity were physical and were most often described as illumination or being in the light. We called this experience of luminosity and being illuminated *illuminosity*. Each person had a different experience of light in transcendence, but it was a recognizable phenomenon.

All the participants described their own experiences of becoming filled with power or light. They described seeing an aspect of themselves they had never known. Their senses became illuminated and clear. They described feeling as though they could see deeply for the first time, or hear intensely for the first time. They told stories of joy, gratitude, and celebration. They had the realization that their bodies were divine. Some people reported feeling as if they could see all around them, as if they could see everywhere. Some people told us that they could see from within a beam of light. Their experiences are similar to experiences of experienced meditators after years of meditation.

A Story of Illuminosity: The Woman Who Saw Her Spirit Dance

Kate, a woman with breast cancer, told us her story:

> I was in the oncologist's office for a bone-marrow aspiration. The test was to determine if my breast cancer had spread to my hip. I had had some hip pain, and the oncologist wanted to find out where it was from. I went into the small examining room and was told to change into a gown. My husband went with me like he usually did and sat on a plastic chair next to the desk where the doctor wrote out his prescriptions. I took off my soft dress. I lifted it over my head and put it neatly on a chair. I knew my husband could see my scar from my partial mastectomy and see how my breast was smaller and had a depression on it, which made it look unlike the other one. My once-beautiful body was now different. My husband often told me that I looked like a warrior, like someone who had been through a battle. I put on the paper gown that did not cover my large body. I was bald from chemotherapy. I had shaved my head when my hair started to fall out, and people told me it looked noble and even elegant. But I wore a wig. Somehow, I was not frightened and I felt at ease.
>
> I had been through this before and more. I was getting good at it. I knew that since my first days after the diagnosis, when it all was dark, when it was like a veil was over my life, I had developed skills and ways of being that were different from who I once was. I could feel my strength, my ability to see who I was, my presence even in this moment. I

walked into the smaller room where the table for the bone-marrow aspiration was. I touched it and, for a moment, sat down on it. I turned away from the table. Now, I was afraid. I was afraid of the pain of the procedure; I saw the size of the needle on the table. I was afraid of the outcome if the cancer had spread.

But as I simply turned away from the table, my body took me. I felt it spin and rise. I stood up in my red leather boots and turned around slowly. As I did this, I raised my arms up and started to spin. I stopped and paused. It was unintentional, an accident. It was as if my arms rose spontaneously. I closed my eyes, then I spun intentionally and raised my arms and closed my eyes and put my head back. I turned and pirouetted and seemed to rise off the ground. I saw myself as a beautiful dancer. I could feel myself starting to spin, to rotate. And as I spun I could feel my spirit rise within me. I could see Her. I could feel Her getting brighter, more powerful than ever before. I was rising off the ground like a spirit. I was soaring, and I was full of light. I was much larger than my body, and the examining room was gone.

And in a moment, I was not afraid of death. I was not afraid of anything. The procedure had receded and did not seem important to me with regard to my spirit. And I spun and twirled and rose and then, to my surprise, I jumped up in the air, threw my head back, and clicked my heels together in a movement of joy and, in a sense, mocking death. I laughed, it was wild, it was not me, I don't do things like that. And then I went back to who I was. I was back in the examining room but different. I was myself. I was calm and energized and strangely happy. I could not have predicted this journey.

Kate's husband told us what he saw:

STEP EIGHT: EXPERIENCE TRANSCENDENCE

She was bald and still looked beautiful. I could see she was afraid and she was starting to get low. And then she spun and rose. For me, I could not see what was happening then. I know it sounds weird, but she seemed to disappear from my ordinary vision, and time seemed to stop. She looked to me to be a woman in a mist, a woman of light, and she rose and looked like Marc Chagall's woman in *The Kiss*. She was up in the air, tilted, colorful, but she was much more like a spirit, like light. And then she did it, she clicked her heels like the woman in the Chagall painting, and the whole room went blank.

For me, it was like the room was full of spirit from all over, and we were inside it. And then it was ordinary and we were who we are. And I looked in her eyes, and I knew even then without thinking about it that I had seen her spirit and that it was so beautiful and that I loved her deeply. And I knew I was in the presence of something much larger than I was and she was. And I was also in the presence of a woman who was really becoming my teacher. This moment was one moment in an ordinary day, but for me, it changed my life. I can see it now as if it were happening again.

Kate told us that while she deals with her fear, her pain, and her impending death, in a moment, she transcends, she experiences illuminosity. She feels her spirit getting brighter.

Illuminosity Brings Enchantment

Within the experience of illuminosity is an experience of images appearing, of beauty and radiance. These new images often showed the person as strong, beautiful, powerful, or healed. The person often felt reborn. In enchantment, a person's senses are awakened anew. The person's body is connected to spirit. Sounds become more intense; the body and its senses become more sensitive. Illumined people feel vitality and recognize it in others. It is described as "the experience of being truly alive." People said that when they are in transcendence, it feels like a gift of their own life. People can feel a vortex of energy around them, which they are part of and merging with. People told us that their senses were so changed that it was a different experience just walking. The colors were so different that they felt the ground was alive and connected to them; they felt oneness.

Illuminosity Shows You Interconnectedness

The visionary artist Alex Grey told us about his vision of transcendence, which changed his life:

> My wife and I lay together and closed our eyes and saw visions as one. One of the first visions was of a mind lattice—a realm of complete interconnectedness with all beings and things via a love energy that was in an infinite, omnidirectional grid, a sort of fountain drain, a toroidal shape. Each being and thing was one of the cells interlocked in this ongoing network. It was there with totally no reference point to the external world or external reality—it was all the energetic realm, and it felt like the total bedrock of reality. This was the scaffolding of creation that the dreamlike world of mundane manifestation was draped over. It felt like a veil had been stripped away, and I was seeing the way things really were. It was beyond time, and it changed my entire point of view about what we are.
>
> I came back from that experience and looked at my wife Allison. She saw the same transpersonal space at the same time that just drove it home to me. I'm not saying that that's it, and that's the only space. But it was my initiation into the mystic headspace that I feel is profoundly true.

STEP EIGHT: EXPERIENCE TRANSCENDENCE

June, a woman with breast cancer, described her vision toward her own healing in this poem:

> Crossing the Beckoning Threshold
>
> I stood timeless
> Places of Wonder
> beholding...
> Golden Sparkles dancing
> Winged Jewels rising
> to adorn the Path Ablaze
> unfolding
> into greater Majestic Light
> restoring
> transforming
> renewing
> becoming
> beheld and yet beholding
> contained and yet containing
> the Mighty One
> the Resplendent
> Presence of Wonder

June writes about her experience of luminosity. She is communicating her vision of standing at the threshold. This poem expresses themes of luminosity common to many participants. She speaks of altering time and space, which she calls timelessness. She speaks of light she calls greater majestic light. She describes the feelings of healing in verbs *restoring, transforming, renewing, becoming*. Finally, she talks of The Mighty One; for her and many other participants in the study, transcendence includes an experience with God or a power greater than themselves. This finding of the patient's experience of God was striking and one of the most interesting themes to emerge from this study.

Visions of the Blessed Mother

Marilyn told us about her first spiritual experience:

> I was a young girl of sixteen. I was in a teenage relationship with a boy I loved, but I knew he was wrong for me. He scared me. When I was with him, I felt like I was on the wrong train and I did not know how to get off. The relationship felt like I was walking down a road into a land that was barren like an empty lot. It got worse. When we were together, the world was distorted and strange. People seemed to me to be hostile and suspicious to us.
>
> To get away, I went on a camping trip with a friend. I woke at dawn and went into a meadow. Suddenly, I saw her in the distance, shrouded in light. It was the Blessed Mother I had prayed to as a child. She walked towards me. I could feel the light illuminating her like a shower of love. It was the most powerful love I ever felt. I knew, no matter how I hurt, she was watching me, taking care of me. In one moment, I knew that even though it was all wrong, somehow I would get through it. That vision or visitation happened in total secret. I have never spoken of it to anyone. I knew then that I was on my spiritual journey. I was lost and this was now my own spirit journey. This was what I had to do to become who I was going to be. She said to me, "I am with you."

In the story, Marilyn is suffering; she is lost. She does not know what to do, and she prays. Then she has a visitation for one split second. All that time, she is alone. Then spirit became illuminated. This story has been told throughout history. Women such as Bernadette have seen the Blessed Mother. Maybe you have, too.

STEP EIGHT: EXPERIENCE TRANSCENDENCE

The Woman Who Was Touched by Christ

Faye had severe rheumatoid arthritis that had left her disabled and had required many surgeries. She told us about a dream. In the dream, she found a veil of water, touched it, and cried. She could not remember the details, but as she told us the story, we could see that she felt it deeply and was very taken by this incident. We had her relax deeply and go into the space that she had learned was her imagery space. We then let her drift. We gave her no guidance; we just comforted her and reassured her by being there with her.

Suddenly Faye started crying. Tears rolled down her cheeks, yet she looked beatific. We let her be there and quietly asked her what she was seeing. She said:

> I am a teenager. I am very frightened. My father is an alcoholic, and I am afraid of him. I run to my room and lie on the bed and cry. I am half asleep. I am drifting in a dream. In my dream, I see myself leave my body on the bed and rise. I am like smoke rising, with my body below.
>
> Suddenly there is a face and a torso and arms. It is huge; it has no size. I know it is Jesus Christ. He is so beautiful. He looks down at me and reaches to touch me. And then he smiles at me and lets one drop of water fall from his fingertips onto my forehead.
>
> That's a ridiculous story, isn't it? I can't have seen Christ. I was so embarrassed by this dream I haven't told anyone until now. In fact, I forgot all about it until I saw it again in my imagery space. It scares me; I don't know what it means; I don't believe in these things. I am not religious.

We told Faye it was all right. We gently took her back into the place where she could see the vision, and we put her back into it. We asked her to slow down time and go in between the moments. We asked her what she felt like, what she smelled, saw, and heard in the slowed-down time. She said:

> His face is surrounded by a beautiful light. He glows. The light comes out of his fingers and goes into my body. It makes me feel tingly, alive. It smells like flowers and electricity. The water or fluid he puts on my face is warm. It goes right through me and fills me with light. It feels wonderful. It makes me sleepy and awake at once. His smile is love. It comes into me and surrounds me. I feel totally cared for and protected.

Faye looked at us, and this time, she was relaxed, not agitated. We asked her whether she could take this memory and feeling with her and keep it. Because she had been there and had a memory of it in her body, could she go there whenever she wanted to? We told her she could go into the vision in between the moments just as she had done when she was a teenager. She could go from darkness to light again.

A year later, her arthritis is in remission. She is no longer disabled; she has moved and started to work in a job that is creative and exciting to her. Her life is new. Her power and strength have returned. She has been healed by her spirit.

Many patients tell of seeing Christ in dreams, seeing him when they were children, seeing him when they are near death. Based on our research, we encourage people who have had experiences seeing Christ to accept the experience and go deeper into their memories of it. The feelings of that vision will help you heal for the rest of your life.

Her Son Appears As an Angel

Lisa, an artist, went into a hospital room to visit a woman and later told us the story:

STEP EIGHT: EXPERIENCE TRANSCENDENCE

The woman lay immobile in her bed. She was hooked up to an IV, which was connected to a central line that went into her chest. She had leukemia and was having a bone-marrow transplant. Her husband sat next to the bed on a plastic chair. He got up and paced the floor and walked like a prisoner from one side of the room to the other. He was like a caged animal, a panther. She cried softly in her pain. Her mouth hurt, she could not swallow from the burning in her throat. She pushed her morphine pump to get some relief. She stared at the blank wall. Her eyes were like dark circles from lack of sleep. The tears had etched lines down her cheeks that were stained from crying.

I came into the room: "I am Lisa, one of the artists from Arts in Medicine. Can I draw for you?" A simple question. Neither the man nor the woman responded. They continued to stare at the wall, and she continued to cry. I started to leave the room. I could hear muffled conversation behind me as I went away. The man came out quickly, almost running. He said to me, "Can you draw an angel?"

I came back into the dark room with its shades drawn and started to draw. The woman sat up, looked at the drawing, she said, "No not like that. Make the hair black. Yes, that is better." She lay back on her bed and closed her eyes. Her face softened. Her eyes closed halfway and became gentle. I continued to draw. The woman now sat upright. She was awake, alert. She spoke as I drew. "Make the face longer, make the nose sharper, put on a white shirt, make the hair shorter." I looked at the woman again. She lay at peace, her face now in a small smile. Her husband held her hand. He rested beside her, his eyes relaxed. The woman started to hum. She started to cry but this time not in pain. She looked off in space as if she was seeing something. She turned her head as if she was listening.

I asked her if the angel was a particular one. I said to the woman, "You seem to know so much about the angel, do you know which angel it is?" The woman looked at me and said, "It is my son. He died in a car accident last year. I have missed him so much. When you came into the room and asked if I wanted you to draw, there was a pause, it was suddenly quiet. An opening appeared in the room in front of me, like a doorway. I heard his voice inside my head. He said, 'Let her draw me, mother.' I was not sure what was happening. I was groggy from my medicines, exhausted from days of crying. I told my husband to call you back into my room, and I told you how to draw him. As you made him come alive, it was as if the room became still. A blanket of stillness came over it and covered the whole room like a mother's care. An energy came over me like a buzzing. I could feel my son everywhere. He spoke to me. 'I am with you, mother, I have always been with you. I will help you heal. I love you.'"

As she said this, tears came to her eyes. Her face looked radiant, as if it was illuminated by a light from within. Her husband cried softly beside her. He held her hand and looked at the drawing, and tears ran down his face in silence.

After that, the woman needed no morphine during her bone-marrow transplant. She mostly slept and seemed to be at peace. She sang prayers often and looked brighter and brighter to everyone who came in. The physicians and nurses on morning rounds could not believe the change that had occurred. It was as if she was inhabited by a spirit, they said. Her blood count improved, and she could now eat. The pain in her throat had subsided, and she now laughed and told stories to her visitors. The drawing of her son as an angel was hung across from her bed, where she could see it whenever her eyes were open. It was the first thing she saw as she awakened and the last thing she saw before going to sleep.

She told me, "He speaks to me always. He protects me always. I know he loves me and I know his love is God's love.

STEP EIGHT: EXPERIENCE TRANSCENDENCE

> I feel like I am in his hands. I don't worry any more about my illness or my treatment. I feel like it is being taken care of by a higher power. I am deeply at peace." The drawing still hangs in the room where she had her transplant. She went home and is doing well. Each patient who moves into the room leaves the drawing up. It is like an angel now protects each person as they come in.

Dancing with the Angels

We spiral to a story we told you in the preface of the book. Now you can see into it more deeply; now it has more meaning. One day, in a bone-marrow transplant unit, a little girl with leukemia dances with the angels. She puts on cloth wings, a flowing silk dress. She spins and whirls and spins and whirls. The dancer sees the little girl's spirit dance. For a moment, the little girl has transcended physical form. She moves in a way that gives her powerful freedom. She can feel her spirit not contained by the body anymore, not trapped in the limitation of her own little body. Her spirit fills the whole room with the spirit of the dance. It happened in an instant, her experience of transcendence.

The little girl's mother tells us the story of her beautiful daughter dancing with the angels. She sits and speaks to us in a dream, surrounded by a heavenly energy, as if it is still happening:

> I am sitting on the edge of her bed. We have been in the hospital off and on for many months, it feels like many years. She is so beautiful when she sleeps, I listen to her breathe. Her body is so tiny and fragile. She gets a little smaller each day. It's been such a long and painful journey. She's my baby, and I love her more than anything. Last year, she was diagnosed with leukemia. We had hoped she was cured. She had all the chemotherapy, weeks and weeks of ra-

diation and finally a bone-marrow transplant. She rallied and was clear. It was a celebration.

During those hospitalizations, Arts in Medicine played a wonderful part in her treatment. The dancer would come in every day; they would throw ribbons around the room and dance, waving their beautiful colored scarves. She loved it and seemed to enjoy it so much. She would giggle and move and flow with the music. She always waited for the dancer to come back. One day, Lisa, the painter, even painted her a T-shirt with her favorite little pussycat on it, who wore her favorite red shoes. She was so proud of that T-shirt, she wouldn't take it off for three days. We made a hat for her bald head that matched her T-shirt. One day, even a musician came in and played her favorite songs: "Twinkle, Twinkle Little Star" and "The Itsy Bitsy Spider." And in the times when she was sickest with her chemotherapy, the musician would come in and just sit on the edge of her bed and sing to her.

It was a really bumpy ride. One day, she was so sick she couldn't do anything; the next, she was better. She is sleeping more and more each day now. We had gone home after a long hospital stay, and we came back for a follow-up to the cancer clinic. We thought we had made it to the other side. Before the doctor even came into the room, my daughter looked in my eyes. She has beautiful brown saucer eyes, a sweet smile. Her hair was sparse, it was just growing back. She said, "Mommy, the bad cells are back." My heart sank, I knew it was over. I knew that now it was just a matter of time.

Later, we were back in the hospital room. It was the last hospitalization, and no one came. The nurses couldn't look into her eyes. Conversations with the residents were short. Her father stared out the window and would not talk. The dancer, the musician, the artist, where had they gone?

The next day, there was a gentle tap on the door. The

dancer asked, "Is she up for dancing?" My daughter's eyes were closed, but just then she opened them. She says, "Oh yes, yes, I want to dance." It was as if at that moment, life returned to her body. The silk scarves waved around her head, the dancer held her body and lifted her gently off the bed. "Maria, would you like to dance with me?" She started, she twirled, she giggled. She floated on the music. It was so beautiful. My precious little girl was dancing. She danced and she danced, and she twirled and she twirled, and I can still hear her soft giggles floating around the room. I could feel the tears rolling down my eyes. It was a precious moment I will hold in my heart the rest of my life.

In the dance, she did a perfect little twirl. And then she paused. She said, "Oh mommy, don't worry about me, I am going to heaven and I will be dancing with the angels." And she did a curtsy, and another twirl. Now the tears rolled down the dancer's face. Maria stood there as the most beautiful little dancer on Earth. She climbed back into the bed, and I tucked the sheets around her. She was so happy and content. I thanked the dancer.

Move from Healing Illness to Healing the Earth

Transcendence is not only about experiences of healing; it is about moving from a place that is focused on the self, to a place focused on others. The experience of transcendence includes seeing God dancing with angels and mystical resonance, but there is also a theme of transcendence that literally transcended people's focus on their own illness.

Many participants moved through their own stories, and they ended up in a place where they were reaching out helping others. Their lives were completely changed. They were moving in a world they never expected. Many of the artists became focused on healing others and the Earth.

Our participants went from being confused and suffering to

being fired up with energy and passion in service to others and the community. They needed to share their visions with others. The healing that takes place is global. It goes from healing a physical illness to healing the Earth.

The Earth Speaks to You

Vijali is an Earth artist who says she heals with the light that comes from within her heart. She told the story of how she went from being a studio painter in Los Angeles to going around the Earth and staying with people and making art to heal. She went to nine countries in seven years in her World Wheel project. In each country, she would ask the people her three questions: "What is your essence? What keeps you from achieving it? (the illness) What would help you be who you are? (the healing)"

Then, with the people she met, she would do an Earth carving or performance piece that embodied the answers to the questions. She would live with the people for months and fall in love with them and with their lives. She would heal them as a community by making the piece with them and sharing in their healing. The Bauls in India needed a community hut to teach the children music, and her art there was for the purpose of building a spiral-shaped music house for the village.

Vijali told us her story of healing the Earth:

> My work right now is global healing. Who am I? I'm just light and space, with red mud splattered on it. When I speak of art, I don't just mean paintbrushes, but the whole of life, where you go, how you sit, how you do everything, everything is part of that gesture of creating. Every thought we have has an effect on the whole galaxy, the whole cosmos, so everything is important, everything is sacred, and everything is ritual. And ritual has an effect on people, so every part of every gesture is having an effect.

There is no separation for me between art and prayer. No, the art is truly the prayer; there is absolutely no separation. When you make a prayer, it is words. The words are vibration or sound, even if you're thinking, and nothing is said out loud. That thought itself is creating a particular vibration, and on some level, even that thought is a sound. The same thing is true with sculpture. As you're carving the sculpture, it's saying something; it is a vibration that is sent out into the world. It is prayer.

Reflections on Transcendence

Create a Sacred Space

Spirit Body Healing takes place in sacred space, a space pregnant with energy and populated with spirits. It takes place surrounded by helpers, angels, voices of God, songs, psalms, prayers. It takes place within beauty, within the Earth, within your body. Sacred space is full of meaning to you. It is the place where spirit enters your life. A church or temple is sacred space if you are an adherent to the religion; a crystal-clear river is sacred if you love nature. Traditionally, sacred space was the place where a religious figure was present or something beautiful in nature was special.

In Spirit Body Healing, we found that sacred space is in your heart. Sacred space is the place where you pray or see visions of God and angels, the imaginary space where you are in contact with your spirit.

You Are the Gift

You yourself become the gift, you become the one who gives each person who you see Darshan. You can make the service happen. Think of ways you can give what you have experienced to others. Start a program in spirituality and healing at a local nursing home, hospital, prison. Join a program already happening: If you are a musician, join a music healing program; a gardener, join a gardening club that helps others.

These illuminated happenings occur throughout your life. Think back on the ones you have had. Close your eyes and see them, feel them, be in them. Let their energy come into you now and see your own spirit illuminated.

Let Yourself Be Seen

It can be frightening to let part of you be seen that has never been seen before. It comes through you, it is mystical. You know it's you, but you have never seen it before. As it emerges, you say, "Is that me? Who is he or she?"

Each part of your life is a gesture of creating, each thought has an effect. Everything is sacred. Every movement has an effect. There is no separation between art and prayer—art is embodied prayer. Prayer is intention to heal, to create the peace of love on a personal level. Everything you do is a gesture in creation, your prayer. Each thing you do is sacred and a ritual. Each thought is prayer and creates vibration like silent sound waves.

Use Guided Imagery

USING YOUR MIND'S EYE
TO INVITE A VISION TO COME TO YOU

Make yourself comfortable. Uncross your legs and arms. Close your eyes, let your breathing slow down. Take several deep breaths. Let your abdomen rise as you breathe in, and fall as you let your deep breath out. As you breathe in and out, you may feel tingling, buzzing, or relaxation. Let those feelings increase. You may feel heavy or light; you may feel your boundaries loosening and your edges soften.

STEP EIGHT: EXPERIENCE TRANSCENDENCE

Now let yourself relax. Let your feet relax, let your legs relax. Let the feelings of relaxation spread to your thighs and pelvis. Let your pelvis open and relax. Now let your abdomen soften, let your belly expand; do not hold it in any more. Now let your chest relax, let your heartbeat and breathing take place by themselves. Let your arms relax, your hands relax. Now let your neck relax, your head, your face. Let your eyes relax; see a horizon and blackness for a moment. Let these feelings of relaxation spread throughout your body. Let your relaxation deepen. If you wish, you can count your breaths and let your relaxation deepen with each breath.

Now imagine that you are in a place that is holy or sacred. It can be a church, a temple, an ancient ruin, a mound, a stone circle, a wonderful place in nature, a waterfall, a mountaintop, a sacred river. You can even picture a place where a person who is sacred to you has had a vision: the mountain where Moses saw God, Lourdes, Jerusalem, Mecca, the tree that the Buddha sat under. Sit for a moment and absorb the energy of this place. Feel all the people who have prayed and had visions before you. Feel the energy of the air, the earth, the water, the fire. See the visions of those who have come before you.

Now ask for a vision to come to you. You are a good person. Call forth a vision for your healing to come to you. Rest for a moment.

Look around you, see that the light is expanding, it is opening. It can be a gray opening the white, or it can be any color you see. Feel how the light radiates from within; feel how the light is light itself, not a reflection of the sun. This light is God's light. Now ask for a vision to come to you. It can be a vision of a deity you believe in, a religious figure you revere, a place in nature where you have had powerful experiences, a teacher, a loved one, an ancestor, whatever spiritual vision you have had in the past that has had the most power.

The vision will appear all around you out of time and space. It can be a presence, a voice, a light, a thought. When you are aware of the presence, listen to what thought comes to you; receive the blessings, healing, support, love, message that the vision brings you. Feel the knowledge of truth and the power the message has. Realize that the message will change your life.

When you are ready, return to the room where you are doing the exercise. First move your feet and then move your hands. Move them around and experience the feeling of the movement. Press your feet down onto the floor, feel the grounding, feel the pressure on the bottom of your feet, feel the solidity of the Earth. Feel your backside on the chair; feel your weight pressing downward. Now open your eyes. Look around you. Stand up and stretch, move your body, feel it move. You are back; you can carry the experience of the exercise outward to your life. You will feel stronger and be able to see deeper. You will be in a healing state. Each time you do the exercise you will be more relaxed and be able to go deeper and be more deeply healed. Now rest in the beauty of the vision. Realize that you can have this experience again whenever you wish.

USING YOUR MIND'S EYE
TO BRING IN THE LIGHT

Bringing in the light is a practice that concentrates light and love in your life. It brings incredible energy to you for healing; it surrounds you with light that comes up from the Earth and down from the sky at once. When you bring in the light, you are also bringing in healing vision; you are calling your spirit to open her eyes and see. As you do the exercise, you will create a dome of light and there will be a vision in the center. Bringing in the light heals you, others, and your surroundings.

When you bring in the light, you are embraced by the love of the universe. You are embraced by the Earth and the healing forces of the Earth. When you bring in the light, God and

STEP EIGHT: EXPERIENCE TRANSCENDENCE

the Goddess see you and love you. Bringing in the light is done with conscious intent. When you are illuminated, you can hear the voice of your spirit clearly, and your intuition sharpens.

This exercise is done outdoors. Go to a place in nature that is special for you. It can be a beach, a clearing next to a beach, a hilltop, a mountaintop, a grove of trees in a forest, a clearing next to a lake, a mound, a stone circle. It can be any place you visit that is sacred to you.

You can do this exercise alone or with another person. If you bring in the light with another person, stand about twenty feet apart, look into the person's eyes, and do it together.

First, pause, give thanks for beauty and for the place. Close your eyes. Put your arms at your side, and relax. Now open your eyes. Slowly, very slowly, raise your arms upward until they almost touch over your head. Now touch your hands together at the top. It is as if you are pointing upward to the sun. As you raise your arms, in your mind's eye sees the light from the sun getting brighter and brighter. It is as if you are creating a sacred dome of light around you. The dome of light rises and rises, and when your arms are together at the top, it is complete. Now slowly bring your hands apart and down to each side. This brings the light down over you and the Earth and holds it there.

Now stand in the light and feel its beauty and brightness. This is God's light on Earth. Look deeper now and see a face in the center of the light. It is the face of a spiritual figure you love. It can be God, the Blessed Mother, the Goddess, or a great spiritual presence.

Now bring your arms to the front of your body and make a cup with your hands. This will bring the love and light into your heart more deeply. Stand in the light and feel its beauty and brightness. This is the light of the Earth. You are receiving a great gift. As you bring in the light, you are loved and cared for, you are beyond time and space, you are deeply at peace.

When you bring in the light, you see and are seen. You are seen by spirit from before, from previous lifetimes, from before time, from everywhere at once. You dissolve and come back together in each stellar moment. It is beautiful beyond belief. When you are seen in the light, you are taken deep into timelessness and spacelessnes. You can feel the energy of your own life, see more deeply than you ever have, and be seen and loved as embodied spirit.

When you bring in the light, you see the face of God, and you are seen by the face of God, infused by life energy. You are truly alive, you feel alive. When you do the exercise with another person, you see the person and are seen. You are seen from many lifetimes at once, you get larger, you see light, immense, sparkling. You bring down the light of the sun, you see God on Earth, bringing in mystical power. When you bring in the light, you raise a mystical energy cone of power. Phenomena happen. When you dissolve and come back in a stellar moment, rest, pause, and be taken by the power of this moment. It is unfathomable, it is huge. Bringing in the light is an experience. Feel it, see what you see; the experience is different for each person. Your experience will be you own.

USING YOUR MIND'S EYE
TO GO FROM DARKNESS TO LIGHT

Let yourself relax, let your breathing slow, go into your place of guided imagery. Rest there a moment, and just be in your breathing. Now remember the most beautiful thing you have ever seen, the most spiritual experience you have ever had, the most intense vision or the most intense religious experience you can remember. Now picture the event more deeply. Feel it in your body. How does it feel? What does it smell like? What does it look like? Is there energy around you? Is there a feeling

STEP EIGHT: EXPERIENCE TRANSCENDENCE

of electricity, a vibration? As you feel yourself slow down, let yourself fall into the spaces between time and space. Rest in the natural pause after you breathe out. You are now within the light, the grace, the place of spirit. You are out of time and within illuminosity, and you are just there. When you have illuminosity, when you have seen it deeply, felt it, drawn it, danced it, sung it, written about it, you will always have access to it.

Now if you wish, you can practice going from darkness into light. For this moment, picture an event in your life that is hard for you. It can be one that is sad or frightening. It can be about an illness you have or have had. For a moment, go into that memory and feel it in your body. Then come back into the experience of light that you felt a minute ago. Now stay in the light for a while. Let it come into you completely, let it wash away the feelings of pain and darkness. If you wish, you can move from the darkness to the light through a passageway or imaginary tunnel. You can move in an instant, as fast as light. You can do this whenever you want to. The first time you do this, choose an image of darkness that you can handle easily. Then later, you can use this imagery to move out of darkness that is more difficult. The light is there for you, and you can go into the darkness of your illness or your fear and then come from there into your experience of light.

USING YOUR MIND'S EYE
TO PRAY ON A BEAM OF LIGHT

This exercise is based on an ancient Tibetan Buddhist meditation called Phowa Practice. To do it, close your eyes and picture a figure that you revere. See the person in front of you, in space, up in the air, with light around the person. See the mists, energy, dots of light around the person. See her or his heart with love coming from it. Then see yourself below in bed sitting where you are. Then picture a beam of light coming from the revered person's heart to yours—and a beam of light coming from your heart to the revered one's. On the beam of light, you can pray. The revered one sends heartfelt prayers down to your heart on the beam of heavenly light, and you send your prayers and thanks to the revered one's heart.

After the visionary experience, you need to come back to the ordinary world, but when your sight returns, you have an enhanced vision, you see with new eyes. In the hero's journey, the seeker needs to come back to the real and ordinary world, to bring back the vision and heal the community, to fix the house. After the journey, however, you are different, the voices you hear in your ordinary world are now different. The voices you heard in your visions can now speak to you always, when you are in your ordinary state.

Restory yourself as one who has seen a spiritual vision. Define yourself as a spiritual person. You can think of yourself in that way. You can tell people about your vision and how you have been changed by it.

USING YOUR MIND'S EYE
TO CROSS THE BECKONING THRESHOLD

Take a deep breath. Close your eyes. Allow your body to relax. Take another deep breath. As you exhale, allow yourself to relax totally. Take these moments for yourself. Relax your head, your eyes, your mouth. Let the muscles around your jaw soften. Relax your shoulders. Let yourself become more and more relaxed. Allow your arms to relax, support your fingers, relax your pelvis. Let the muscles around your eyes relax. Feel your whole body relax.

Now, with your mind's eye, imagine you are on a threshold. Let time stand still. See that it is a place of wonder. See golden sparkles within you dancing. See jeweled wings rising. In the path in front of you unfolds a majestic light. See the light surround you. Let it restory, transform, renew you; let it reclaim

STEP EIGHT: EXPERIENCE TRANSCENDENCE

you. You are in the presence of wonder. See the creative spirit within you rise. You can make the impossible possible. You can do whatever you wish. Behold the majestic one, you are in the presence of wonder. *You are.*

Relax deeply, breathe in and out slowly, and let your belly rise as you breathe in and fall as you breathe out. Now listen to the silence that surrounds you. Go into the presence that is caring for you. It may sound like a buzzing of bees at a great distance. Look at the light that comes from inside the silence. You can start by looking at the light outside and then look at the light inside you. Feel the light in your chest as relaxation, feel the light opening you. The magic light comes into you from somewhere or someone, and—as with a massage—it opens your heart. Take several deep breaths. As you breathe in, feel the space around you open. See the space open further and further as if the walls of a huge stadium were being pulled away. See the space expand until you are in a place where there are no limits. Now feel a sense of expectancy, a waiting that has a noise to it like a soft rain. From within the opening light, from within the soft, even background noise, feel a presence, a voice, a power. You will hear it and think it at once. The presence or information will come from within you and outside of you at once. It comes from everywhere and has been there forever. It is speaking directly to you. It is the voice of God.

PART THREE

The Spirit Body Healing Method

Chapter 12

The Prescription for Spirit Body Healing

Starbursts within the Stories Reveal Wisdom

Spirit Body Healing is a method for finding the unique and individualized way of healing for each one of us. From the stories, we have made a simple eight-step method that you can use to heal your own life, whether you are ill or are dealing with a life crisis. The Spirit Body Healing method will become a personal guide to awaken and illuminate your spirit.

The steps will not always go in this order—often they are mixed or even happen all at once. The process is not linear; it is a spiral. Some people do not do all of the steps, and concentrate on some steps more than on others. Some people go right to transcendence without spending much time in darkness. For everyone, however, the process is simple, not complicated. The method is not rigid; it is a guide. It will be different for each of you.

Each subsection in this chapter is a prescription. It is a prescription from a physician and a nurse. Like a prescription for a medicine, fill it and take it. Imagine that these steps are written on a prescription pad by a physician. They are—by you.

Step One: Go into Your Own Pain and Darkness

Prescriptions for Dealing with Pain and Darkness

Breathe

Breath deeply and slowly, relaxing your entire body. Breathing is an anchor. In the moments of immense pain, your breath holds you grounded in your body. Breath infuses the pain with space and your life force.

Meditate

Meditation is not difficult to learn and use for healing. It creates a focused concentration that allows you to be clear and be centered. You can do a walking meditation, a dance meditation, a swimming meditation, or yoga. There are many techniques to facilitate the meditative experience. Find one you are at home with. It is simple. You can meditate by painting, writing poems, or doing gentle and slow activities. In meditation, you go to a place within, which is connected to your breathing. Your movement emerges naturally.

Discover how to meditate

Find a quiet, comfortable place in your home, where you will not be disturbed. Give yourself time, ten or twenty minutes when you do not need to do anything. Sit on the floor on a small pillow in a yoga posture with your legs crossed under you and your hands crossed in your lap, or sit on a straight-backed chair. Allow your body to relax, and focus on your breathing. Watch your breathing; pay attention as you breathe in and out. When thoughts come in, let them go. Return to your breathing. When you feel sensations in your body, return to your breathing. Simply pay attention and breathe. Softly, slowly, allow yourself the luxury of nothing. Be in silence. As thoughts come into your mind, simply let them go, returning to focus on your breath. Your meditation will deepen with time and practice; it is very simple.

Face your pain

Tell the story of your pain to someone you love and trust. It can be a friend, a healer, a family member, a religious advisor, a support group. When you tell the story, make it vivid with imagery, so the other person can feel it and see through your eyes and so that you become connected to another person.

Make art with the story of your pain and darkness. Paint your pain, draw it, write a poem about it. You will capture the essence of how dark it was or is for you.

Look deeply at your pain; let it be a reflection. Go into your feelings. Look at all aspects of it, all causes, abandonment, losses, fears; go into the feelings. If you can, do it with the help and support of those you trust and love. This can be difficult.

If you have an illness, deal with your prognosis. What did the doctor say? Restory the statistics to allow for your own individuality, for magic, and for miracles. Remember, if a physician tells you statistics about recurrence, they apply to populations, not individuals. Even if you were told you had a ten percent chance of being cured, when you are cured, you are one hundred percent cured.

Restory your illness

Make your story positive. Re-create words to define your experience. A woman with breast cancer told us that she called her medical team her "boob squad" and reworded her entire experience to be positive, humorous, and hopeful. She called her radiation therapy the "magical beam of healing light." Make a problem a challenge.

Live with music

Allow yourself to flow on the rhythms of sounds. Allow the vibrational energy to merge with your pain and reverberate within your body. The pain may intensify and then begin to dissipate.

Talk about your fear of death

Do not avoid thinking about death and talking about it. Dealing with death and dying is beneficial. David Spiegel, at the Stanford Medical School, studied women with metastatic breast cancer who were in support groups. He found that women in support groups lived twice as long as women without support groups. He found that talking about death and facing death was one of the most useful parts of the support process. People with cancer often have difficulty talking about death to people who do not have cancer. They need someone who is in the same situation, who can feel what they are going through.

Extract your pain

Merge with the pain, and allow your body to be in union with it. Move into it, make sounds into it, let it take you to a place where it bursts. Release and give birth to it. Be physical. Allow it to move through your body.

Concentrate on something to hold your focus

Watch a movie, meditate on a mandala, make a piece of art. To release yourself from obsessive thoughts about pain, you can count breaths and meditate. This starts you on your healing journey; it starts you going elsewhere.

Create a sound of very deep humming from deep in your chest. Use the vibrational energy to fill you. You can also do repetitive chanting to focus, or you can say a repetitive prayer.

Connect with water

When you are in pain, despair, anxiety, go into water. Water is the element that is emotional and moving—it swirls around us, takes us into Earth's body. Water is fluid spirit. Spirit moves and needs fluidity. Sometimes, we need to immerse ourselves and then float, carried in the water, filled with the abandonment of lack of gravity. The energy and connection with water is powerfully healing.

Affirmations for Pain and Darkness

Repeat to yourself these affirmations:

> It is useful for me to face my pain and darkness.
> Darkness is my doorway to healing.
> Darkness is my doorway for my stronger self to emerge.
> Darkness is the doorway to beauty and light.

Step Two: Go Elsewhere

Prescriptions for Going Elsewhere

Facing pain and darkness takes you elsewhere. It is as if concentration and looking at who you are brings you to a place where you are the witness and you can see. That place is not the place of your pain. Elsewhere is the discovery of freedom from the thoughts of illness that are difficult to control.

Go elsewhere to nature

Nature gives you gifts that are beyond imagination. A herd of elk at sunset on a ridge is a gift. A peregrine falcon diving for a mouse and picking it up right in front of your eyes is a gift that can take you elsewhere.

Find places around your home where you can go elsewhere. Find sacred places in nature, springs, waterfalls, mountains, lagoons, the ocean.

Go for walks alone or with friends. Walks are a constant in almost all the stories in this book.

Experience sunsets or sunrises—you can see heaven's light in the sunbeams and the afternoon shadows.

Dream and daydream

Dreams are your teachers. Remember your dreams, ask for them, write them down as soon as you wake up. Keep a dream journal.

Translate your dream into reality by making art. Keep a journal, paint, draw, sculpt, dance, sing, and tell a story to someone about what happened to you in your dream.

Let yourself daydream. Spend hours doing nothing. As you daydream, ask for healing daydreams to come to you, ask for your spirit to speak to you in your daydreams. Daydreaming is a common characteristic in almost all our participants' stories.

Take the information from your daydream and act on it. Use it to guide you and tell you what is in your heart. A healing daydream is your spirit speaking. As Vijali says, "Honor those little feelings that float up."

Use your imagination

Create a fantasy world that is a safe place. Populate it with helpers, animals, people who protect you and guard you. You can be your own character, like a character out of a novel. You can create helper characters. In this space, you can do anything you want.

The creation is much richer if you make art to make it real. Draw, even stick figures. Cut out pictures from magazines if you do not want to draw. Keep a journal, write about it, intentionally make it richer. Art will take the material, and without your trying to do anything, art will make the imagery healing. The story or the painting will bring healing figures into itself. Art is one of the most powerful ways of inviting spontaneous healing images to appear.

Create rituals

Nighttime or early morning periods are sacred for yourself. You can pray, light a candle, take a bath. Do things that slow you down and put you in an altered state. The in-between space between being asleep and out in the world is your own.

Invite the trigger to go elsewhere

Look for your trigger, your invitation to go elsewhere. Ask for it to come. Have an attitude of watchful waiting. Be patient.

A person may invite you to do something new and creative. It could be an invitation to read a book, go to a movie, make art. Consider it an invitation, and respond.

Watch for synchronicity and coincidence. If an event happens over and over again, it may be a message to you. If you see an advertisement for a painting class, and then a friend invites you to paint, and then you get a painting kit in the mail for your birthday, this might be a message to you from the universe to try something new.

Be a guardian at the threshold of your mind

In making each moment count, it helps to shut off things that are toxic. Whatever it is that makes you upset—the news, newspapers, television—shut it off, put it away. Allow your body to teach you what it does not want to be connected with. Information can be painful. Stories of people dying can be painful. Your mind is the sacred space that your spirit fills. It is up to you to see what comes into it and what you do not expose yourself to. Movies are often the fantasy of someone trying to make money with sensationalism. News is often presented purposely to raise ratings rather than to educate.

Learn to see the invisible

The spirit is first invisible. Allow yourself to pause, go elsewhere, slip into a space where what once was invisible becomes visible. The invisible becomes accessible to us in daydreams; fantasy allows the spirit to spawn. It often helps to eliminate incoming information. By eliminating overload, you allow your spirit to flow. If too much is coming in, you can't see inward; there needs to be silence. In all the stories, our participants stopped too much outside input; they all went elsewhere. They all shut off the television and radio and let the world recede. That is when they found God and saw spirit.

Going Elsewhere Affirmations

Going elsewhere takes me away from my pain.
Going elsewhere is going to my safe place where I am protected and can be myself.
Messages to take me elsewhere will come to me if I listen.
Within a pause, the timeless silence of going elsewhere takes me.

In my dreams and daydreams, I can go elsewhere.
An inner voice will speak to me and take me elsewhere.

Step Three: Find Your Own Turning Point

The turning point is moving into a creative space. Turning point is about dealing with the obstacles, dealing with the fear, returning to what is true for you. In your turning point, you allow yourself to go and become your true self. Turning point is movement and change. In your turning point, you can remember what you wanted to do and do it, even if it takes changing your life. Choose a new path if the path you are on is not working for you. Start from where you are, and move to where you will be.

In your turning point, you do an activity to help you hear the voice of your spirit speaking. When you do activities to illuminate your spirit, you will become open and will be spoken to. The activity could be a garden, a prayer, art. The more you do, the more the experience will become real and grow. If you are making art, the series of pieces will allow you to see deeply and change. These voices or images that you will see will be from your own life. You will get ideas, visions, dreams, jokes, voices, and do something to make them real. The turning point is the place of deepening.

Prescriptions for the Turning Point

Begin the turning point, start a turning-point activity now. Start gardening, using humor, helping others. Reflect on the stories of people from our studies. Take a lesson from our participants, and make art: No matter what else you do, write, draw, paint, sculpt, keep a journal, dance, play, and listen to music.

Follow your bliss to your turning point

To pursue a creative process, do what you are most interested in. Do whatever has pure electricity for you, follow what you love. Follow what is compelling.

Go into it, merge with it, pay attention to thoughts that tell you you are on the right path. Do things to keep the process alive. Do anything, buy things, start projects, get materials, try many different things without worry about failure.

Pay attention to what you are learning as your eyes open and you receive ideas. Pay attention to new body feelings of enhanced sensations. Look for signs of your own strength and healing, and concentrate on them.

Creativity research has shown that the best ideas come after you do the work and then let the problem go. Researchers found that walks let information come to you when you are relaxed. It is the pause that allows your creative mind to work unfettered by worry and anxiety.

Go to places of beauty. Drive to an overlook, and watch the sunset, the sunrise. Go to the ocean, to an arboretum; visit English gardens, walk in beautiful landscapes. Hike to springs, waterfalls, art museums; look at Monet's *Waterlilies*. Landscapes allow you visual space and embrace you in beauty. Take a deep breath, go to a place of deep beauty, go there and rest. Go deeply into the beauty. Look into the center of roses, listen to the sounds of birds, go fishing for hours, silently wait for things to come to you.

Meditate, walk, disengage. Do what you love to do. Do what you desire, what you have always wanted to do. Fall in love, take a friend to Italy, take flying lessons, make a quilt. Doing what you have always wanted to do is the turning point. Leave your work as an accountant, and become a ballet dancer.

Let it grow

When you find an activity, do not hold back. Go for your dream. Do it in steps, one at a time, let it grow by itself. Wait for ideas to come telling you what to get into. If you have no idea, go to what was the last thing you did in your life that you loved, even as a child. Get into it completely, make it an interest that grabs you and is powerful enough to hold you tight. Feel your interest and passion as body sensations; honor them and get into them. Realize what is happening, and make it grow.

As your interest expands, don't stop there, find new interests, new media, new things to do. Let your mind fly, let dreams that seem impossible happen. The more ill you are, the less you have to lose. Get people around you to help if you are too ill to do it yourself. They will see this as a gift they will never forget.

Look within the process for spirit and prayer, for light, and grab it. Make the next piece of art, or take your next step. Look at what you just did, to find the most brightness or the part of what you did that attracts you most, and make the next step from there. Move toward the light. Have the goal of healing and growth behind the whole process. Let the process be the healer. You do not have to do anything or understand in words what is happening.

Draw on turning-point resources

Use books to learn how to reclaim your inner artist. Our book *Creative Healing* will teach you how to use a variety of media to heal. Art, music, dance, and writing are all ways of healing. *The Artist's Way* by Julia Cameron shows you how to use art and spirituality to heal. Meditate fifteen minutes daily; listen to guided-imagery tapes with music. Create a time to be still and quiet. Allow your inner creative nature to emerge. The turning point is the dawning of the new day, the place where the seed bursts open. Take walks in nature, in your neighborhood, which facilitate a contemplative state of mind. Walks give you a moment of thoughtfulness, space to daydream, and the curiosity to discover and explore.

Make art as a turning point

Find art materials that you are attracted to. It does not matter if you do not know how to use them. Look through magazines, or daydream, and find an image that grabs your attention, one that echoes how you feel. Then start painting, writing, dancing, playing music. Allow yourself to get excited about the physicality of what you are doing. Feel the colors of the paint, see how the shapes appear on the canvas. See what you are making, see how it echoes your feeling, where you are. Forget about thinking about how you felt. Instead, *look* at how you felt. Get excited about the making of the art, the process of painting, writing, dancing. Then get another canvas, and start a series. Be free. It does not matter what you do, there is no critic, it is only about healing. Realize that you are painting your life.

Next, create a studio space for yourself, and simply continue your creative work. In the beginning, make no attempt to define yourself or your process. Make art from pure feeling states. Become absorbed in the pure expression and gesture of the process.

Completely release your energy passionately on the art. Then, release this image, step back, look and see what you have created. You will see an aspect of yourself that you can face and let go of.

Let your art be physical. Embody your pain as you paint it. This lets you experience your pain in a new way. You are in control, and you are the creator of your new self. There is movement, and you are witnessing your own transformation.

Making art is an embodiment, using touch, vision, hearing,

smell. It releases ancient memories. Symbols emerge that are an ancient language.

Do repetitive tasks such as basket weaving, where you touch and move over and over again. Hear inner voices as songs over and over again. Inner voices often repeat like a mantra. Create mantras for your own healing. Take what your inner voice says to you, and repeat it over and over again as you do a task that is repetitive.

In making art, do not be defeated by adversity. If you cannot make a pot on a wheel because your hand is paralyzed, make a slab. Mystical destiny may be taking you to a place you cannot have chosen on your own.

See the artist's light, see like a photographer. See light in the early morning and late afternoon. Photographers shoot many of their pictures in the moments after dawn and before sunset. The colors are rich and warm, the shadows long and dramatic. They shoot in moonlight, full moons.

Make a series; each one will grow from the one before. In making the next one, look for something that attracts you in the last work, then go from there. Pick the place of highest energy, brightest color. If you want to move toward the light, make your next piece from the brightest part of your last. If you need to follow and explore the darkness, make your next piece from the dark imagery.

Do not worry about understanding what the images are, what they mean, how they are healing. Simply trust it all, and it will happen from your unconscious.

Take a pilgrimage to a sacred site to heal

When you go on your pilgrimage, your goal is to have a vision, an embodied experience. If you are going to a sacred spring where a nun saw a vision of the Blessed Mother, you can see through the eyes of the nun and see the Blessed Mother, too.

When you get to your pilgrimage site, do a deep-relaxation

exercise to invite a vision to come to you; say a prayer. Then close your eyes and wait for thoughts to come to you from the person who saw the vision at the site or from the sacred personage who appeared in the vision. It feels like a daydream, like your own thoughts—but clearer. Let the figure speak to you, listen to what the figure tells you. You can ask questions about your illness, treatments, or healing. You can say a prayer and visualize a beam of light between the figure's heart and your heart.

Plan your own healing ritual or ceremony

Spirit increases with the number of people who are present. A healing ritual or ceremony is a way of bringing people together with the intent to heal. Do not be frightened by the word *ritual*. What you do need not be formal, religious, or New Age. It can be as simple as eating lunch together with your closest friends or going to a meditation retreat for an evening with someone important to you.

To plan your own healing ritual, first think about what you need to be healed. Go for a walk, meditate, slip though the veil, and let an image, thought, or voice come to you. Try to see in your mind's eye a ceremony that will be beautiful and healing for you. It can be anything. Our patients have told us stories of women's groups, moon groups, men's groups, trips to places in nature (such as springs), religious services, almost anything. One woman with cervical cancer had all her woman friends come to her home and cover her with rose petals and sing to her. Many participants told us that pain disappeared during and after the ceremony.

Dream it, get friends to do it for you, with you. Take pictures, and keep a journal; record it so you can make it part of your healing story.

Use music, sing, chant, hum, or drum to raise energy. Use

costumes, candles, altar pieces, art, and sacred things you have found to make your experiences more embodied and real.

Make a healing circle

When you are in a healing circle, you can feel the love and the healing energy moving and magnifying. To make a healing circle, invite friends and people you love to come. Let them surround you and then pray for your healing. They can sing and chant, tell you they love you, speak or be silent. They can hug you as a group or stay where they are and pray. They can picture white light, picture you well, picture spirits or healing presences coming through them.

Dance with your demons

Do a dance, and let the darkness come out; release it. Do a physical act as you do the process. Allow your body to express release in the dance or ritual.

Reclaim the shaman within

Have a vision you want to turn into, see what you want to be, and create it in the world. Make a piece of art of what you will turn into.

Affirmations for the Turning Point

I can be creative to heal.
I am beautiful and talented and can do whatever I wish.
The creative fire will emerge from deep within me.
The creative spring flows from my heart forever.

The basic affirmations for the turning point are

I am an artist, I am an artist.
I am an artist who uses art to heal.

Step Four: Slip through the Veil

Suddenly, you are within your own body in a place of spaciousness. You can have a dream of God, see the Buddha, feel an experience of enlightenment. Slip through the veil into the place of opening. Move out of pain and see your spirit dance. Slip through the veil, and glimpse angels, saints, grandparents, or ancestors. You will find yourself suddenly curled up in God's hands, held and comforted. Slip through the veil into the place of the shift of consciousness that is the place of deep healing. The shift starts with going inward, but here it happens for real. When you slip through the veil, you go into a deeper state than when you went elsewhere. Go to the place where the spiritual experience lives and is accessible. Go to the other side, where the spirit is visible.

Prescriptions for Slipping through the Veil

Slipping though the veil is a magical moment, and it happens in an instant. In truth, it cannot be prescribed. We can only suggest ways to find an opening within you that will allow you to recognize this moment. Knowing it is possible and that it is within you is the way.

Take your spiritual history

What ways of slipping through the veil are already known to you? Did you do natural childbirth, have you been in a trance, have you done meditation, yoga? Have you done church retreats, women's support groups, religious ritual and ceremony, Catholic visions, listened to saint stories? Your spiritual history, the story of your illness, and the story of your skills are very important now. Take an inventory of what you have done in your life, which prepares you to go deeper.

Honor the spiritual experiences you have had

The memories of them will resonate within you and take you to a place that is fertile. For example, if you remember a moment when you saw an angel, go back to the experience; feel it in your body again. Feel your awe when you were surrounded by the light. Feel the place that you were in between worlds. Go back to the lived experience, remember it. Make it more than a memory, make it a spiritual experience available to you now. That is the threshold in between worlds.

What books have you read that have given you information that you will use on your journey? On a healing journey, there are inner teachers and outer teachers.

Go through your memory bank. Look at photographs, images, quilts that tell you who you are. Read old love letters. Dream.

It's intense on the other side. Dams break, there is speaking in tongues, you are deeply taken, it is very dreamy and nonordinary. It is about oneness and connectedness.

Do guided imagery to take you deep into another world.
Make a fantasy world, and populate it with characters.
Make art about what you see on the other side.

Affirmations for Slipping through the Veil

Inside the veil, I see beauty.
On the other side, I am myself.
Inside, I will see angels appear, light appears.
Inside is a different place; I will see the darkness open to lightness.
I will meet spiritual beings as helpers.
Inside, I am in a place where I am cared for, loved, and held.

Step Five: Know the Truth and Trust the Process

In this step, you will know that you are flowing in a process that is beyond you and is taking you. You will know the truth of what you are seeing; you will feel the validity of the visions and voices within you.

Prescriptions to Know the Truth and Trust the Process

Generate movement quickly

Keep the flow moving; do one act after another quickly. The doorway out of one act is the entry into the next one.

Expect surprise

Trust the process; it grows. A process is one step at a time. It is much larger than you are. You cannot imagine what will happen if you do what you love and trust the process. It comes from spirit, from the heart of the living Earth.

Direct the process

Only you know what you need to heal. When the teacher comes, ask for what you want, tell the teacher what to do, make your wishes clear, and do it. Trust your teachers, though. You will know when to trust them, you will know when they know more than you do, when their knowledge and experience are just what you need.

Remember that synchronicity and chance are healing teachings about trust

When you are ready, information will come to you from everywhere. Anyone can be your deepest teacher. Do not judge a person by external characteristics; a man at a gym or a sales clerk could be the one with exactly what you need. A person in an elevator, a man in a car-rental agency, a woman in a class you are taking—each could be your healing teacher. Be open minded, in search constantly, alert like a hunter for a word that could change your life. Your body sensations help you know you have found a teaching. You feel out of space and time, in a trance, different.

Try not to be impatient

Insights come after long periods of nothing happening. Days or weeks can precede the insights. Insights come after hard work, long periods of trying to solve a problem in your mind or work. Wait for the insight to come. It is waiting for the truth. Truth is a whole system of belief, coherent and meaningful; truth comes together with time. The pieces of the puzzle appear one at a time, then suddenly you see the whole and gasp. It is a feeling not a theory. Finding the truth requires doing something. It can come to you unbidden, but it most often comes after a great deal of work.

Hear your own inner voices of the truth

When your spirit speaks to you as an inner voice, you have thoughts that are like your ordinary thoughts except they are clearer, more focused, and sound slightly different. They may have a new cadence, an accent, a new way of speaking. The distinction is subtle. Ask for your spirit to speak to you, then listen and pay attention to the thoughts you are having. If your mind wanders, bring it back. If you are having thoughts about your illness or problems in your life, bring your mind back to what your spirit is telling you. Do not worry or put yourself down when your mind wanders; this is natural. But bring it back and then pay attention to the spirit's clear messages.

Your goal is to be able to receive a clear coherent message that has a teaching and a theme that you can remember and use in your life. It takes practice; it will happen. As you listen to your inner voices more and more, you will be able to understand them better and to understand their language as they call to you in the physical world.

When you see a spiritual vision, look at it deeply, look at it sideways. Be attentive to thoughts and feelings you have. Listen to the inner voice speaking to you. You will have thoughts that are unusual, you will suddenly feel as though you are slightly out of space and time, and you will feel different. This is the experience of your spirit becoming illuminated.

All information we receive is through our thoughts, our bodies, our emotions. The place below words is power and then art. We can feel it, and then dance it, draw it, sing it, tell its story, and only then describe the experience in words.

Use your own life as a studio to create something bigger than you

To solve a problem in your life or to get answers to what you are seeking, let go. Go on a walk. After you have spent time trying to solve the problem, just walk. The answer will come, maybe today, maybe next week. Look and see the answer, invite something more to come to you, allow yourself to see it. Trust yourself to listen to your own voice. Follow your own instincts without understanding. Allow yourself to become a vehicle for something to come through that is greater than you are. The walk and letting go will allow you to tap into the wellspring of your own eternal creativity. It is a way to allow your own life to be painted on a canvas, or in the words of a poem. Go to a place inside yourself you have never been before. Let yourself go deep within. Inside yourself is the vibrant creative passion itself. In the darkness, it is scary and frightening. The illness and its suffering take you down to a place inside yourself where something more emerges.

Trust that you will find something that will be perfect and fabulous, frightening and exhilarating at the same time. It will be so alive that it will represent your life. It is not planned, it is meant to be, it is destiny. What you will do will become your destiny. You will fly on the wings of your destiny. Close your eyes, take a deep breath. Something much bigger than you is coming through, something greater within your own self. It can come from the thing you are doing, from your art. You don't need to go outside yourself to find your answer. When you make something, let go, allow it to happen. You become a vehicle for something greater than yourself to happen. It is revealed to you in the piece of art itself. You let it happen; the thing comes to you and makes you whole. You are healed by it. Do what you are supposed to be doing.

Affirmations for Knowing the Truth and Trusting the Process

I know the truth.
I am at home.
I know I will get well.
Healing is a flow.
I let go of my inner critic.

Step Six: Embody Your Own Spirit

Embodiment of the spirit is about merging. Let images of beauty and radiance appear to you. See yourself as strong, beautiful, powerful, or healed. Feel reborn as a brand new person. Feel enchantment; feel your senses awakened anew. Let yourself feel sounds becoming more intense, feel your whole body and its senses be more sensitive. Feel vitality, and recognize it in others. This feeling is described as the experience of being truly alive. When you are in the world, feel alive in world. Receive the gift of your own life. Feel a vortex of energy around you, which you are part of and merging with. Let yourself see and feel images of light and beauty; immerse yourself in the enormous feelings of healing. Experience body sensations of energy, buzzing, vibration, calmness, joy. The sensations feel wonderful.

Prescriptions for Embodying Spirit

Be with beauty

See beauty in the person you are working with, see beauty in yourself. When you are seen with beauty and compassion, love is born. Feel love for the other. Then the candle in your own heart lights and expands, and the other can feel it.

Go in between the moments

To see deeply into a spiritual vision, see between the moments, between the spaces. It is like slipping into time and space. Slow it all down, look carefully at the vision. To go in between the moments, look at an event again from within a moment of stillness. It is like freezing time, letting it slow down and finally stop completely. Then look and feel the event fully inside the moment of stopped time. A metaphor for looking between the moments is looking down at your hand and opening the fingers. If your fingers are the moments of time, when you spread them apart, the spaces between them are like the experience of going in between the moments. They are the spaces in between time, where there is no time. In that place of stillness and peace, that place of altered consciousness, you can see into the event more deeply than you remember. You can see energy, love, peace, visions, and feel the experience deeply in your body.

Make your life a prayer

Each interaction is deeply sacred, for within each moment, you see pure embodied spirit.

Imagine that your every act is done to enhance the spirit of every living thing

Imagine that you are a sacred one, like the Dalai Lama. Go into a room. How will you be? Imagine that the god or goddess is within you; imagine that he or she is coming through you, and you are the goddess or god on Earth. How will you be? When you see someone with embodied spirit, you fall in love with God. You love the person as you love God, you feel a deep spirit around you, you see beyond time and space. Everyone can embody spirit. It is simply who you are. To see it, all you need to do is fall in love. See through the personality into who the person truly is. You can fall in love with yourself and see your own embodied spirit.

Merge with something

Embodying spirit is about merging completely with something, being one with it, seeing through its eyes, using all your senses to be there. Move toward it. Go toward the beauty. Use your outer senses first, then allow yourself to get dreamy. Then your inner senses will come into play. Then they will join and both be there at once. You will move from yourself to what you are merging with. Slip out of your body, go into the flower. Now feel it. Use both your senses and your imagination. When you are within a magnolia flower, you are both seeing it from the outside and seeing from within it at once. Close your eyes, get dreamy, then listen for thoughts that come to you from across the veil.

Cultivate awareness

Cultivate the awareness of the presence of your own spirit. Cultivate the awareness of seeing another's spirit. You see a glow of light around them, you see beauty in the sadness of the moment. Spirit Body Healing involves cultivating a sensitivity to see beauty and light in each person in every moment.

Practice Spirit Body Healing

Spirit Body Healing takes constant, deliberate, intentional thinking about things, as you may never have thought about them before. It is taking spirit and blending it with the ordinary. Spirit is there with us; we don't have to go to spirit. Our beauty is seen inside the pain. You can still see the pain for yourself and others. Spirit moves in, out, around; spirit is bigger than we are. The body holds it; it is larger than our lives, larger than we thought it could be.

Affirmations for Embodying the Spirit

> My heart is open.
> I love you.
> You are beautiful.
> I am beautiful.

Step Seven: Feel the Healing Energy of Love and Compassion

Spirit Body Healing is about feeling compassion for yourself. You go to a place where you restory your life from compassion and love. When you see yourself with compassion, you can tend to your body as a sacred body, tend to emotions as natural forces that move though you. You can honor intuitions and insights, you can be illuminated to find your place in the world. Spirit Body Healing is about feeling healing energy. When you feel the energy of the universe flowing through you, you will heal.

Prescriptions for Feeling Healing Energy and Compassion

Go into body sensations as your guide

When you can see and feel in an enhanced way, do more and more of it. If you see your baby's hand for the first time, pay attention to it, journal it, paint, it, tell it as a story. Honor the event and make it real.

See yourself from afar

Become compassionate for yourself by seeing yourself from a distance, from outside. Stand back and say, "Look at her (or him). She (or he) needs this." In a moment of witness, of reflection, see what you need to heal.

Let down your boundaries

Compassion is a kind of love; it joins your light with another's. If you are ill, it joins you to the healer; if you are a healer, it joins you to the person you are healing. When you are in compassion, you flow beyond your boundaries and merge with the person you are with. You see the person without judgment, you see the person with God's love. You see this person as beautiful, as sacred; you see the person's spirit instead of her or his personality.

Healers who see with compassion see their patients in a different way. If you are ill, and you see those around you with compassion, you invite them to see you in this way, too. Your love is felt by everyone and helps them love you with compassion, too.

Show your light in compassion

Imagine a light within you that is glowing. Imagine that when you are being healed, the light goes out of you and merges with the light of the healer and all of those around you. Imagine it magnifying and getting brighter and brighter.

Stop judgment

To cultivate an experience of healing energy and compassion, stop judgment. In your mind's eye, imagine your heart opening.

Shift your breath

Experience a vibrational shift into deep breathing. Open again, be present. Move into a place inside yourself where you feel patience. Relax, allow time to become infinite. Listen to the story, focus on your own experience of awareness. Feel a surrender that has a vibrational quality. Everything slows down, and you become quiet. There is a vibrational quality of the moment in becoming one with your breath.

Concentrate on body sensations

To feel healing energy, first become aware of your body. Concentrate on your sensations. Relax by using the guided-imagery exercise given in Chapter 10. Pay attention to feelings of buzzing, vibration, tingling, and numbness. When you feel these sensations, focus your whole mind on how they feel in your body, where they are most intense, what the actual sensations are. Do so over and over again until you know what the feelings of relaxation feel like to you in your body.

Pay attention to your body as you have your own experience of slipping though the veil and embodying spirit. Notice the feelings of tingling and buzzing that accompany your spiritual visions and peak experiences.

As the peak experience comes to you, notice what happens as it approaches. Many people glimpse it in advance, and when they see it coming, their bodies feel different than usual. Notice feelings of purification or cleansing. Be aware of how the energy seems to fill you up. Then, after the feelings of healing energy, see whether these feelings seem to be followed by deep feelings of being at peace. Notice changes in your breathing.

Affirmations for Feeling Energy and Compassion

I feel the healing energy of buzzing, vibration, calmness, joy.
I feel compassion for myself, I love myself.
I feel compassion for others, I love others.

Step Eight: Experience Transcendence

The major goal of Spirit Body Healing is for the reader to experience transcendence. The experience of a peak spiritual event is possible for anyone who wants this to happen. Everything in this book leads up to experiencing transcendence. Going into the darkness, slipping through the veil, feeling energy—all are steps to hear and see visions of pure spirit.

Transcendence is about experiencing feelings of oneness, an immense interconnectedness. It is about emerging into another dimension, one of great power and beauty. In the Spirit

Body Healing study, transcendence often involved hearing a message from God.

Experience transformation, see yourself for the first time, discover within yourself a place of ecstasy. Let yourself become filled with power or light.

Transcendence also involves sharing. You are a vehicle to share love, to communicate love. Transcendence is doing right action in service to heal the Earth.

Prescriptions for Experiencing Transcendence

Make your life an embodied prayer

Your spiritual work is your embodied prayer. From the first glimpse of spirit from within your pain, your entire healing journey is an embodied prayer. Each act is part of your prayer for your healing, part of your prayer of thanks, part of your prayer to heal others and the Earth.

Invite a hallucination

Let your eyes cross, let a shape that is in natural forms trigger a memory of a creative idea from inside you. This is how the artist works—artists get ideas from shapes. The sculptor sees a piece of wood and gets the idea of the animal he carves from the grain pattern. He sees it in the wood. The hallucination is the spiritual vision.

When a vision appears, let yourself see it.

Let yourself see beauty, let yourself see spirit. Seeing a vision is letting go, accepting, honoring, inviting.

Go into other places without time and space

Feel the place of no space and no time. Timelessness is a feeling.

The space has characteristics. Certain visions are seen by many spiritual people or meditators. Cracking, sizzling, opening areas, light, flames, borders—all are common. When you look at spirit, look for these things. When you look at paintings of religious themes, you see halos, flames, light rays.

Look at the work of visionary artists

Artists such as Alex Grey spend their whole lives painting spiritual visions of transcendence. His portrayal of space is close to what patients who are near death tell us they see: lines of electricity, lightning, areas of white light, jewels. Look at pictures of God or religious figures painted by visionary artists. Collect sacred art and sculpture, and place them around you. Put them where you can see them when you wake and go to sleep. Take them to the hospital with you. Listen to sacred music, make altars.

Go into nature

In the silent fog of dawn is pure spirit manifest. Go into the actual energy, into the opening light.

Commune with another

When you are ill or if you are a healer, merging with another is a powerful healing tool. When the love and light that are within you merge with the love and light from another person, it magnifies and deepens and becomes extraordinarily powerful.

If you are sick, let yourself expand and flow outward to the healer or people who are healing you. You can make a healing circle to magnify the energy even more.

Be mindfully present

Experience awakening to the sacred, awakening to nature, involving smell and touch, moving through space and time. This experience involves a shift in your ability to see.

Pray

To create sacred space to heal in your life, say a prayer. Give thanks to the god you believe in. Ask the spirit you believe in to come to you and help you heal. You can make an altar, a medicine wheel, a place where you put a painting, to give you a tangible place to start.

Open your inner eyes

With your eyes closed, see the light that comes from within. As you feel yourself slip across the veil, as you feel time and space changing, be aware of the appearance of the moment of peace out of time. Look for it with beauty. As you feel it coming, it seems as if space opens, expands, changes quality. It is subtle if you have not experienced it before, and each time, you learn to recognize it more easily. For most people, a soft light appears, a voice or vision appears and speaks. You may have an intuitive understanding and knowledge that it is God, that you are in the presence of God.

The knowledge is a deep understanding. It is an experience, not a theory. Notice your intense feeling of timelessness, peace, eternity. It feels as if you are in another dimension.

Glimpse God, glimpse angels

Experience the power of the universe or God. Feel yourself in the presence of God, and hear the voice of God. You have every right to see and experience the voice of God, angels, Jesus, the Blessed Mother.

Crucial to having the experience is letting it come to you without extinguishing it with fear or judgment. If you believe it can happen to you, it will; if you think it can only happen to saints, you will not allow yourself to accept the vision when it starts to come.

Look especially for the experience of illuminosity, the experience of the light within and without as one. It is described as a radiance from within itself, not from the sun. It can be as much a feeling as a vision.

When you see or hear the voice or vision, there will be a message. You will often receive a message from God to you about how to heal and who you are and what to do, not just experience a vision.

It often helps to create an event where spirit will enter, where transcendence will appear. Dance, music, art, prayer, nature all make it more likely. A ritual you perform alone and a ritual repeated with other people also make it more likely to happen.

SEE THE BLESSED MOTHER

Imagine you are walking at dawn in a beautiful meadow. In the distance you start to see a vision—it is a woman shrouded in light. It is the Blessed Mother. See her walk toward you. Feel the light radiating from her like a shower of love. It is the most powerful love. Know that no matter how you hurt, she is watching you, taking care of you. In one moment, know that no matter what is happening, somehow you will get through it. You are on your spiritual journey. She says to you, "I am with you."

QUIET DOWN TO HEAR THE VOICES OF THE SPIRIT

To hear the inner voices of your spirit, it is essential to quiet down. You need to create a mystical silence away from the material world, where you call these voices and invite them to come.

Take a walk, paddle on a river, hike in the mountains, then let your eyes drift, your ears listen for any sound. When you see a shape, like a cloud, let it form into a vision. Listen with your inner ear, not to sounds. See within your inner eye, not sights. There is a pause, a moment of rest, then you can hear an inner voice. It will sound like your own thoughts but different—clearer, more straightforward, like listening to a voice with its own character.

You need to be lost to be found, you need to be a seeker to find, you need to ask for a spiritual vision to come to see God. When you are ill, you are looking for healing, your priorities change, you are open. When you are ill, you are like a vacuum waiting to be filled with spirit. When you are ill, you are an invitation to spirit to enter. When you are in darkness, you are an invitation for light to come in. It is not something anyone wants, but once it is here, you can turn it into your way to spirit.

Listen for thoughts inside yourself. To hear inner voices, honor them, listen, do not be a critic. When you are ill, you ask questions, "Why am I like this? What can I do to get better? What caused my illness?"

DO RIGHT ACTION IN THE WORLD

Spirit Body Healing is about moving to a place of consciousness to do right action in the world, which benefits the whole. Do work that is healing to yourself and others. Let your work honor and respect the sacred nature of life.

Affirmations for Experiencing Transcendence

I feel a oneness and interconnectedness with all beings.
I am surrounded by gods and angels.
I will share and teach what I have experienced.
Illuminosity surrounds me.
As I heal myself, I am healing the Earth.

Chapter 13

The Teachings from the Edge

*Raise the Storyteller
to the Level of the Wisdom Keeper*

Honor each experience, and embody each one as you go through your own journey of healing. Take your desire to be healed. Embody the experiences that are the path of healing. Have faith that spirit flows within you. God is in there, the angels are there within this experience, and there is faith, hope, and transcendence.

These teachings came from the stories. You will recognize them from the stories you have read throughout the book. As we read them, we remembered, too. Here are the teachings to help you embody experiences of healing.

Learn the Teachings from the Edge

See the face of God around you. He will speak to you. If you look, you can see the light that comes out of his hands. Praying to God makes you feel as if you are blessed and beautiful. After you pray to him and see him, you will know.

When you make art, ancient spirits come to you and speak to you. They are all around you and will be there forever. They tell you who you are and support you.

Expressing your pain will allow you to release it. This expression will allow you to get control of your life and move forward. Making art will give you the gift of the vision of who you are.

Throw your whole life into it. Commit to it.

There is a spirit inside you. It looks like a dove; it loves you and is full of energy.

Concentrate on beauty; it will take away your pain.

Look right into the face of your deepest fear; it will speak to you, and you will let it go.

Go right into your pain, let it be there, let the space around it grow. You will feel better.

Go into nature; listen. The ancient spirits are all around you; they will speak to you and tell you what to do. Do it, then your power will come back, and you will do service for others and be new.

Follow your daydreams; listen. A voice will come to you: follow the voice. You will be new; your life will be changed forever.

You are part of the divine.

There is a safe place you can go that is around you always.

Around you are thoughts that come like light beams and change your life.

Beauty is all around you; it is all sacred and magnificent as it is. Listen to it, and see it.

Inside you is a healer that will heal you and everyone around you.

In your dreams, you can see the dead, ancestors, gods, spirits.

You are surrounded by energy connected to everything in a grid.
There is nothing to fear.
You will become what you see.
In a flower is perfect beauty. If you go there, you will feel the love that surrounds you and takes care of you forever.
There is no time.
The darkness within you will leave, and then you will heal.
People in your life who have died are all around you and, as angels, they will touch you and heal you.
There are animals around you that can heal you.
Those you love are as spirits around you and can heal you.
Under your deepest fear is always love.
Do something, make art, and sudden knowledge will come to you.
The air around you is full of energy.
Near death is perfect peace and love.
Love is a gift you can give and share. You can hand it to someone at your death.
Dreams are powerful teachers of spirit.
Angels and guardians surround us and come for us when we die.
Grace is right there within softness.
You are full of beauty right now. Can you see it?
Love and prayer are gifts that can come to you in a sunrise.
Within you is an energy of healing, a life force.
Compassion for yourself is a way of seeing.
Different spaces and times are around us to go into altered states.
Each person is surrounded by visible light and energy.
All people are visible in their most beautiful state right now, at any age, timeless.
God is around you and will speak to you.
The Blessed Mother takes care of you.

Christ takes care of you.
Now it all fits together perfectly.
Each gift goes with all the others.
Accept each gift.
Look and see who you are.

Carry one of these teachings with you as you go through your day. Remember the story where the teaching came from. Let the teachings that are meaningful to you be your gift from our research study.

Epilogue

✸

I Close My Eyes in the Darkness

The voice of God speaks to you.

> I close my eyes and this is what I see.
> I am in the darkness.
> I am confused, suffering, and in pain.
> I am grieving, ill, depressed.
> In this situation, I am very uncomfortable.
> It is almost unbearable.
> I feel contracted.
> It's extremely dark.
> I need help.
> I want to make things better.
> I must take action.
> I kick, I squirm, I move, I spin.
> I feel pain in my entire body.
> I want to burst out of here.
> I want to go to a place totally different.
> Suddenly, it becomes tighter and tighter.
> I can't breathe, my chest hurts.
> The walls are closing in on me.

I am about to go on a journey.
Everything in my life will change.
I am seeking.
I am searching.
I see a silver cord that leads to a star.
I see that I am somehow attached to it.
I am totally alone, I have a vision.
The vision is powerful.
I feel it with my entire body.
I yearn for it.
I hear a voice.
I hear a song.
I see an extraordinary light.
I have never seen this light before; it is still only a glimmer.
The vision is so shadowy, it is mysterious.
I am moving into the totally unknown.
Suddenly, my body begins to spin.
Am I singing?
It is my song.
Am I moving, spinning? Is it my dance?
Something has happened; I have become entranced.
My attention is grabbed.
I am going elsewhere.
I cross a membrane; I move and slip through a mystical veil.
Gasp. Now I am on the other side.
Here it is all different.
It feels like a dream.
It is a visionary place
where time and space have changed,
colors are enhanced,
my senses are full,
I am surprised.
I hear and see things.
It is beautiful. I know it is the truth.
I hear a voice emerge from within:

You have found yourself.
Look and see who you are.
See yourself with love and compassion, even if it is for the first time.
When you look back into the past, it will be a new story.
You have found the memories from before. See it with love.
You have made a new life.
You are singing, you are dancing,
You have re-created yourself and your life.
You are merged with my spirit.
You are an illumination of the life force.
Feel your breathing slow.
My touch is healing you.
You are embodied spirit and embraced in love.
In this new body, you will see more deeply.
You will receive visions and messages from a force that is greater than yourself.
Each day, you will know me better.
You have been seen with the greatest love.
Each day, messages will come to inform you and heal you.
You have become yourself.
Your life is now about who you are.
You are deeply connected to the ones around you, the ones you love.
You are part of my kingdom and the Earth.
You have a vision of a new life.
On this healing journey, you have been reborn.

The voice of God is speaking to us in this last meditation. The voice of God came through this story. Close your eyes. Go into your pain. You are being born into something new, you are an illumination of spirit. Life is full of suffering, pain, and death—but there is rebirth.

Recommended Reading

✴

Achterberg, J. *Woman as Healer.* Boston: Shambhala, 1992.
Achterberg, J. *Imagery and Healing.* Boston: Shambhala, 1985.
Achterberg, J. *Using Imagery For Health & Wellness.* New York, 1994.
Adams P., and Mylander M. *Gesundheit!* Rochester, VT: Healing Arts Press, 1998.
Ader, R. *Psychoneuroimmunology.* New York: Academic Press, 1981.
Aldridge, D. "An Overview of Music Therapy Research," *Complementary Therapies in Medicine* (1994).
Amonite, D. W. "The Role of Art Therapy as an Emotional Support System for HIV/AIDS Related Issues," International Conference on AIDS, July 7–12, 1996; 11, no. 2, 428 (abstract no. Th.D.5155).
Antonovsky, A. "A Sense of Coherence as a Determinant of Health," J. Matarazzo, ed., *Behavioral Health*, New York: John Wiley & Sons, 1984.
Arieh, S. *Creativity: The Magic Synthesis.* New York: Basic Books, 1976.
Audette, Anna Held. *The Blank Canvas: Inviting the Muse.* Boston: Shambhala, 1987.
Baldwin C. *Life's Companion: Journal Writing as a Spiritual Quest.* New York: Bantam Books, 1991.

Bandura, A. "Catecholamine Secretion as a Function of Perceived Coping. Self-Efficacy," *Journal of Consulting and Clinical Psychology* 53, no. 3 (1985): 406.

Berk L. S., Tan S. A., Fry W. F., et al. "Neuroendocrine and Stress Hormone Changes During Mirthful Laughter," *American Journal of Medical Science* (1989): 298, 390–396.

Bertman, S. L., ed. *Grief and the Healing Arts: Creativity as Therapy*. Amityville, NY: Baywood, 1999.

Block, J.; Swanson, J.; Mott, J. R.; and Wallace, C. *The Healing "I."* Gainesville, FL: The Write Solutions, 1992.

Blofeld, J. *The Tantric Mysticism of Tibet.* Prajna Press, 1970.

Bolle, K. *The Bhagavadgita.* University of California Press, 1979.

Borysenko, J. *Minding the Body, Mending the Mind.* Boston: Addison-Wesley, 1987.

Breslow, D. M. "Creative Arts for Hospitals: The UCLA experiment," *Patient-Educ-Couns.* 21, no. 1–2 (June 1993): 101–110.

Bruck, L. "Nursing Care: Artists in residence," *Nursing Homes*, 43, no. 7 (September 1994): 50–51.

Brunner/Mazel, Levittown, PA, 1994.

Byers, J. F., and Smyth, K. A. "Effect of a Music Intervention on Noise Annoyance, Heart Rate, and Blood Pressure in Cardiac Surgery Patients," *American Journal of Critical Care* 6, no. 3 (May 1997): 183–91.

Cameron, J. *The Artist's Way: A Spiritual Path to Higher Creativity.* New York: Tarcher/Putnam, 1992.

Cameron, Julia. *The Vein of Gold: A Journey to Your Creative Heart.* New York: Tarcher/Putnam, 1996.

Campbell, D. *The Mozart Effect.* New York: Avon, 1997.

Campbell, Don, *The Roar of Silence.* Wheaton, IL: Theosophical Publishing House, 1989.

Campbell, J. *The Hero With a Thousand Faces.* Princeton, NJ: Princeton University Press, 1990.

Campbell, J. *The Inner Reaches of Outer Space.* New York: Alfred Van Der Marck, 1986.

Campbell, J. *The Masks of God: Primitive Mythology.* New York: Penguin, 1976.

Campbell, J. *Myths to Live By.* New York: Bantam, 1973.

Campbell, J.; Eisler, R.; Gimbutas, M.; and Muses, C. *In All Her Names*. New York: Harper-Collins Publishers, 1993.

Cassou, Michell, and Cubley, Stewart. *Life, Paint and Passion: Reclaiming the Magic of Spontaneous Expression*. New York: Putnam, 1993.

Castaneda, C. *The Eagle's Gift*. New York: Pocket Books, 1981.

Caudell, K. A. "Psychoneuroimmunology and Innovative Behavioral Interventions in Patients with Leukemia," *Oncology Nursing Forum*, 23, no. 3 (April 1996): 493–502.

Chodorow, Joan. *Dance Therapy and Depth Psychology: The Moving Imagination*. New York: Routledge, 1991.

Cornell, Judith. *Drawing the Light From Within: Keys to Awaken Your Creative Power*. Wheaton, IL: Theosophical Publishing House, 1997.

Cousins, N. *Anatomy of an Illness*. New York: Bantam/Norton, 1979.

Cousins, N. *Head First: The Biology of Hope*. New York: Dutton, 1989.

Covington, H., and Crosby, C. "Music Therapy as a Nursing Intervention," *Journal of Psychosocial Nursing and Mental Health Services*. 35, no. 3 (March 1997): 34–37.

Csikszentmihalyi, M. *Flow: The Psychology of Optimal Experience*. New York: Harper & Row, 1990.

Dienstrey, H. *Where the Mind Meets the Body*. New York: Harper, 1991.

Dossey, L. "The Rediscovery of the Mind," *Advances* 5, no. 3 (1988): 73.

Dubois, J. M.; Bartter, T.; and Pratter, M. R. "Music Improves Patient Comfort Level During Outpatient Bronchoscopy," *Chest: The Cardiopulmonary Journal*, 108, no. 1 (July 1995): 129–130.

Edwards, Betty. *Drawing on the Right Side of the Brain*. New York: J. P. Tarcher, 1989.

Eliade, M. *Myths, Dreams, and Mysteries*. New York: Harper & Row, 1957.

Eliade, M. *Rites and Symbols of Initiation*. New York: Harper & Row, 1958.

Eliade, M. *The Sacred and the Profane*. New York: Harcourt Brace & World, 1957.

Eliade, M. *Shamanism.* Princeton, NJ: Princeton University Press, 1972.

Eliade, M. *The Two and the One.* New York: Harper & Row, 1969.

Eliade, M. *Yoga, Immortality and Freedom.* New York: Pantheon, 1958.

Emunah, R. *Acting for Real: Drama Therapy Process, Technique, and Performance.* Brunner/Mazel, 1994.

Erikson, E. *Childhood and Society.* New York: Norton, 1950.

Evans-Evans Wentz, W. Y. *Tibetan Yoga and Secret Doctrines.* New York: Oxford University Press, 1958.

Fawzy, I. et al. "Malignant Melanoma: Effects of an Early Structured Psychiatric Intervention Coping and Affective State on Recurrence and Survival Six Years Later," *Archives of General Psychiatry* 50, no. 681:9.

Fox, J. *Finding What You Didn't Lose: Expressing Your Truth and Creativity Through Poem-Making.* New York: Tarcher/Putnam, 1995.

Fox, J. *Poetic Medicine: The Healing Art of Poem-Making.* New York: Tarcher/Putnam, 1997.

Fox, M. *The Coming of the Cosmic Christ.* New York: Harper & Row, 1988.

Fromm, E. *The Art of Loving.* London: Mandala, 1957.

Fry, W. F. "The Respiratory Components of Mirthful Laughter," *Journal of Biological Psychology*, 19 (1977): 39–50.

Fry, W. F., and Salameh, W. A., eds. *Advances in Humor and Psychology.* Sarasota, FL: Professional Resources Press, 1993.

Gablik, S. *The Re-enchantment of Art.* New York: Thames and Hudson, 1991.

Gardner, Kay. *Sounding the Inner Landscape.* Stonington, Maine: Caduceus Publications, 1990.

Garfield, L. M. *Sound Medicine: Healing with Music, Voice and Song.* Berkeley, CA: Celestial Arts, 1987.

Ghiselin, B. *The Creative Process: A Symposium.* Berkeley: University of California Press, 1953.

Goldberg, Natalie. *Writing Down to the Bones.* Boston: Shambhala, 1986.

Goldberg, Natalie. *Living Color: A Writer Paints Her World.* New York: Bantam Books, 1997.

Goldstein, J. H., and McGhee, P. eds. *Handbook of Humor Research*. New York: Springer Verlag, 1983.

Good, M. "Effects of Relaxation and Music on Postoperative Pain: A Review," *Journal of Advanced Nursing* 24, no. 5 (November 1966): 905–914.

Graham-Pole, J.; Lane, M. R.; Kitakis, M. L.; and Stacpoole, L. "Re-storying Lives, Restoring Selves: The Arts and Healing," *International Journal of Arts Medicine* 4, no. 1 (1996): 20–23. Also presented at IJAM Symposium, June 22–25, 1995, Gainesville, FL.

Grey, Alex. *Sacred Mirrors*. Rochester, VT: Inner Traditions International, 1990.

Guzzetta, C. E. "Music Therapy: Hearing the Melody of the Soul," in Dossey, B. M., et al., *Holistic Nursing: A Handbook for Practice*, 2nd ed. Gaithersburg, MD: Aspen Publisher, 1995, pp. 669–68.

Hall, H. R. "Hypnosis and the Immune System," *Journal of Clinical Hypnosis* 25, no. 2 (1983): 92.

Halprin, Anna. *Moving Toward Life*. Wesleyan University Press, 1995.

Harner, M. *The Way of the Shaman*. New York: Bantam, 1982.

Harvey, A. *The Way of Passion: A Celebration of Rumi*. Berkeley, CA: Frog Ltd., 1994.

Henry, L. L. "Music Therapy: A Nursing Intervention for the Control of Pain and Anxiety in the ICU: A Review of the Research Literature," *Dimensions in Critical Care Nursing* 14, no. 6 (November/December 1995): 295–304.

Highwater, Jamake. *Dance Rituals of Experience*. New York: A.W. Publishers, 1978.

Hoffman, J. "Alternatives: Complementary therapies. Turning in to the power of music," *RN* 60, no. 6 (June 1997): 52–54, 57.

Homan, S. "The Theatre in Medicine," *International Journal of Arts Medicine* III (1994): 26–29.

Ivker, R. and Zorensky, E. *Thriving*. New York: Random House Inc., 1997.

Jacobson, E. *How to Relax and Have Your Baby*. New York: McGraw-Hill, 1965.

Jahn, G. *Margins of Reality*. New York: Harcourt Brace Jovanovich, 1987.

Johnston, K., and Rohaly-Davis, J. "An Introduction to Music Therapy: Helping the Oncology Patient in the ICU," *Critical Care Nursing Quarterly* 18, no. 4 (February 1996): 54–60.

Johnstone, K. *Impro: Improvisation and the Theatre.* New York: Routledge, 1992.

Jung, C. *Man and His Symbols.* New York: Doubleday & Co., 1964.

Jung, C. *Memories, Dreams, Reflections.* New York: Vintage Books, 1961.

Justice, B. *Who Gets Sick.* New York: Tarcher, 1987.

Kabat-Zinn, J. *Wherever You Go, There You Are.* New York: Hyperion, 1994.

Kaminski, J., and Hall, W. "The Effect of Soothing Music on Neonatal Behavioral States in the Hospital Newborn Nursery," *Neonatal Network* 15 (1996): 45–52.

Kandinsky, W. *Concerning the Spiritual in Art.* Translated and with an introduction by M. T. H. Sadler. New York: Dover, 1977.

Kaptchuk, T. J. *The Web That Has No Weaver: Understanding Chinese Medicine.* New York: Congdon & Weed, 1983.

Klaus, M., and Kennell, J. *Parent-Infant Bonding.* New York: C.V. Mosby, 1982.

Kobasa, S. "Personality and Constitution as Mediators in the Stress-Illness Relationship," *Journal of Health and Social Behavior* 22:368.

Krupp, M. *Current Medical Diagnosis and Treatment.* Norwalk, CN: Appleton and Lang, 1997.

Lane, M. T. "Model of Creativity," in P. Chinn, ed., *Art and Aesthetics in Nursing.* New York: National League for Nursing, 1994.

Lane, M. T., and Graham-Pole, J. "Development of an Art Program on a Bone Marrow Transplant Unit," *Cancer Nursing* 17, no. 3 (June 1994): 185–192.

Lane, M. T., and Graham-Pole, J. "The Power of Creativity in Healing: A Practice Model Demonstrating the Links Between the Creative Arts and the Art of Nursing," *NLN Publ* 14, no. 2611 (June 1994): 203–222.

Lee, R., and DeVore, I. *Kalahari Hunter-Gatherers.* Cambridge, MA: Harvard University Press, 1976.

Lefcourt, H. M., Davidson-Katz, K. et al. "Humor and Immune-

System Functioning," *International Journal of Humor Research* 3 (1990): 305–322.

Lelievre, D. "Art Therapy Support Groups Conceived in an Integrative Way: A Global Approach for Reinforcing Self-Esteem of People Living with HIV/AIDS," International Conference on AIDS, July 7–12, 1996, vol. 11, no. 1 (abstract no. Tu.D. 2851): 406.

LeShan, L. *Cancer as a Turning Point.* New York: E.P. Dutton, 1989.

Levine, S. *Meetings At the Edge.* Doubleday and Co, 1974.

Levine, S. *A Year to Live: How to Live This Year as if it Were Your Last.* New York: Bell Tower, 1997.

Lewis, C. S. *The Four Loves.* Orlando, FL: Harcourt, Brace & Co, 1960.

Lindsay, S. "Music in Hospitals," *British Journal of Hospital Medicine* 50, no. 11 (December 15, 1993–January 18, 1994): 660–662.

Lingerman, H. A. *The Healing Energies of Music.* Wheaton, IL: Quest Books, 1995.

Locke, S. *The Healer Within.* New York: New American Library, 1986.

Lovelock, J. E. *Gaia.* New York: Oxford University Press, 1979.

Luthe, W. *Autogenic Therapy.* New York: Grune & Stratton, 1970.

Lynn, D. "Healing Through Art Therapy," *Journal of the American Art Therapy Association* 12, no. 1 (1995): 70–71.

Magill-Levreault, L. "Music Therapy in Pain and Symptom Management," *Journal of Palliative Care* 9, no. 4 (Winter 1993): 42–48.

Maisel, Eric. *Affirmations for Artists.* New York: Jeremy P. Tarcher/Putnam, 1996.

Malchiodi, C. A., ed. *Medical Art Therapy with Adults.* London and Philadelphia: Jessica Kingsley, 1999.

Malchiodi, C. A. "Medical Art Therapy: Contributions to the Field of Arts Medicine," *International Journal of Arts Medicine* 2, no. 2 (Fall 1993): 28–31.

McIntyre, B. B. "Art Therapy in Hospice Care," *Caring* 7, no. 8 (August 1988): 48–49.

McKinney, C. H.; Tims, F. C.; Kumar, A. M.; and Kumar, M. "The Effect of Selected Classical Music and Spontaneous Imagery on

Plasma Beta-Endorphin," *Journal of Behavioral Medicine* 20, no. 1 (February 1997): 85–99.

McNiff, S. *Art as Medicine: Creating a Therapy of the Imagination.* Boston: Shambhala, 1992.

Metzger, Deena. *Writing for Your Life: A Guide and Companion to the Inner Worlds.* San Francisco: Harper, 1992.

Miro, J. Je Rêve D'Un Grand Atelier. Paris: XX Siecle, 1938.

Muktananda, S. *Meditate.* State University of New York Press, 1980.

Nachmanovitch, S. *Free Play: Improvisation in Life and Art.* New York: Tarcher/Putnam, 1990.

Nightingale, F. *Notes on Nursing: What it is and What it is Not.* London: Harrison and Sons, 1859.

Oldham, J. "Psychological Support for Cancer Patients," *British Journal of Occupational Therapy* 52, no. 12 (December 1989): 463–465.

Ornish, D. *Love and Survival: 8 Pathways to Intimacy and Health.* New York: Harper Perennial, 1998.

Ornstein, R., and Sobel, D. *The Healing Brain.* New York: Simon and Schuster, 1987.

Oyle, I. *The Healing Mind.* CA: Celestial Arts, 1974.

Pelletier, K., and Herzing, D. "Psychoneuroimmunology: Toward a Mindbody Model," *Advances* 5, no. 1 (1988): 27.

Pennebaker, J. W. *Opening Up: The Healing Power of Expressing Emotions.* New York: Guilford Press, 1997.

Perlis, C.; Wallace, D.; and Rosenbaum, E. "Sharing the Patient Experience in the Classroom with the Art for Recovery program." Proceedings of the Annual Meeting of Social Clinical Oncologists 13 (1994): A 1552.

Pert, C. B. *Molecules of Emotion.* New York: Scribner, 1997.

Pert, C. "The Wisdom of the Receptors: Neuropeptides, the Emotions, and Bodymind," *Advances* 3, no. 3 (1986): 8.

Poole, W. *The Heart of Healing: The Institute of Noetic Sciences.* Atlanta: Turner Publishing, Inc., 1998.

Robinson, V. M.: *Humor and the Health Professions: The Therapeutic Use of Humor in Health Care.* Thorofare, NJ: Slack, 1991.

Roche, J. "Spiritual Care of the Person with AIDS: Literature and Art Can Touch Closed Hearts," *Health Progress* 73, no. 2 (1992): 78–81.

Rogers, Natalie. *The Creative Connection.* Palo Alto, CA: Science and Behavior Books, 1993.

Rossman, M. *Healing Yourself.* New York: Walker and Co., 1987.

Sabo, C. E.; and Michael, S. R. "The Influence of Personal Message with Music on Anxiety and Side Effects Associated with Chemotherapy," *Cancer Nursing* 19, no. 4 (August 1996): 283–289.

Sambandham, M.; and Schirm, V. "Music as a Nursing Intervention for Residents with Alzheimer's Disease in Long-term Care," *Geriatric Nursing* 16, no. 2 (March/April 1995): 79–83.

Samuels, M. "Art as a Healing Force," *Alternative Therapies in Health and Medicine* 1, no. 4 (September 1995): 38–40.

Samuels, M. *Art as a Healing Force: An Essay.* Bolinas, CA: Bolinas Museum Catalog, 1993.

Samuels, M., and Lane, M. R. *Creative Healing.* San Francisco: Harper, 1998.

Samuels, M., and Lane, M. R. *Path of the Feather.* New York: Putnam, 2000.

Samuels, M., and Samuels, N. *Healing With The Mind's Eye.* Summit Books, 1990.

Samuels, M., and Samuels, N. *Seeing With the Mind's Eye.* New York: Random House-Bookworks, 1975.

Samuels, M. and Samuels, N. *The Well Adult.* New York: Summit Books, 1988.

Samuels, M., and Bennett, H. *Be Well.* New York: Random House-Bookworks, 1974.

Samuels, M., and Bennett, H. *Spirit Guides.* New York: Random House-Bookworks, 1973.

Samuels, M., and Bennett, H. *The Well Body Book.* New York: Random House-Bookworks, 1972.

Samuels, M., and Bennett, H. *Well Body, Well Earth.* San Francisco: Sierra Club, 1982.

SARK, *A Creative Companion: How to Free the Creative Spirit.* Berkeley, CA: Celestial Arts, 1991.

Schneider, J.; et al. "The Relationship of Mental Imagery to White Blood Cell (Neutrophil) Function." Uncirculated mimeograph, Michigan State University College of Medicine, 1983.

Schroeder-Sheker, T. Music for the Dying: A Personal Account of the New Field of Music-Thanatology–History, Theories, and Clinical Narratives, *Journal of Holistic Nursing* 12 (1994): 83–99.
Siegel, B. *Love, Medicine & Miracles*. New York: Harper & Row, 1986.
Simons, T. R. *Feng Shui Step by Step*. New York: Random House, 1996.
Simonton, S., and Simonton, C. *Getting Well Again*. New York: Bantam, 1978.
Sonke-Henderson, J. "Healing Through Art," *Women's Health Digest* 2, no. 4 (1996): 330–331.
Sourkes, B. M. "Truth to Life: Art Therapy with Pediatric Oncology Patients and Their Siblings," *Journal of Psychosocial Oncology* 9, no. 2 (1991): 81–96.
Spear, W. *Feng Shui Made Easy*. SanFrancisco: Harper, 1995.
Spiegel, D.; Bloom, J. R.; Kraemer, H. C.; and Gottheil, E. "Effect of Psychosocial Treatment on Survival of Patients with Metastatic Breast Cancer," *Lancet* (1989): 888–891.
Spiritual Fulfillment Through Creating. Boston: Shambhala, 1995.
Standley, J. *Music Techniques in Therapy, Counseling, and Special Education*. St Louis: MMB Music, 1991.
Standley, J. M.; and Hanser, S. B. "Music Therapy Research and Applications in Pediatric Oncology Treatment," *Journal of Pediatric Oncology Nursing* 12, no. 1 (January 1995): 3–8; discussion 9–10.
Stern, R. S. "Many Ways to Grow: Creative Art Therapies," *Pediatric Annals* 645 (1989): 649–652.
Sundaram, R. "In Focus: Art Therapy with a Hospitalized Child," *American Journal of Art Therapy: Art in Psychotherapy Rehabilitation and Education* 34, no. 1 (August 1995): 2–8.
Swimme, B. *The Universe Is a Green Dragon*. Santa Fe, NM: Bear & Co., 1984.
Tart, C. *Altered States of Consciousness*. New York: Doubleday and Co., 1972.
"Thanatology–History, Theories, and Clinical Narratives," *Journal of Holistic Nursing* 12 (1994): 83–99.
Toombs, S. K. *The Meaning of Illness*. Norwell, MA: Kluwer Academic Publishers, 1993.

Ulrich, R. S. "View Through a Window May Influence Recovery from Surgery," *Science* 224 (1984): 420–421.

Updike, P. "Music Therapy Results for ICU Patients," *Dimensions of Critical Care Nursing* 9 (1990): 39–45.

Updike, P. "Through the Lens of the Artist-Scientist: Reflections for the Pediatric Oncology Nurse," *Journal of Pediatric Oncology Nursing* 7, no. 1 (1990): 4–8.

Van Manen, M. *Researching the Lived Experience.* Washington, DC: Human Science for an Action Sensitive Pedagogy, 1990.

Walker, C. "Use of Art and Play Therapy in Pediatric Oncology," *Journal of Pediatric Oncology Nursing* 6, no. 4 (October 1989): 121–126.

Warren, B.; ed. *Using the Creative Arts in Therapy: A Practical Introduction.* 2nd ed. New York: Routledge, 1997.

Watkins, G. R. "Music Therapy: Proposed Physiological Mechanisms and Clinical Implications," *Clinical Nurse Specialist* 11, no. 2 (March 1997): 43–50.

Wilhelm, R. *The Secret of the Golden Flower.* New York: Routledge & Kegan Paul, 1969.

Woodman, M. *Addiction to Perfection.* Toronto: Inner City Books, 1982.

Worlds. New York: HarperCollins, 1992.

Wyngaarden, J. *Cecil Textbook of Medicine.* Philadelphia: W. B. Saunders, 1996.

Ziesler, A. A. "Art Therapy—A Meaningful Part of Cancer Care," *Journal of Cancer Care* 2, no. 2 (April 1993): 107–111.

Zimmerman, L.; Nieveen, J.; Barnason, S.; and Schmaderer, M. "The Effects of Music Interventions on Postoperative Pain and Sleep in Coronary Artery Bypass Graft (CABG) Patients . . . Including Commentary by Miaskowski," *C Scholarly Inquiry for Nursing Practice* 10, no. 2 (Summer 1996): 153–174.

References

Allen, P. B. (1985). Integrating art therapy into alcoholism treatment. *Amer. Journal of Art Therapy, 24*(1), 10–12.

Arieh, S. (1976). *Creativity: The magic synthesis.* New York: Basic Books.

Bachelard, G. (1969). *The poetics of space.* Boston: Beacon Press.

Bailey, S. (1997). The arts in spiritual care. *Semin. Oncol. Nurs. 13*(4), 242–247.

Bertman, S. L. (1991a). Bereavement and grief. In H. Green (Ed.), *Introduction to clinical medicine.* Philadelphia: B. C. Decker.

Bertman, S. L. (1991b). *Facing death.* New York: Hemisphere.

Blair, F. (1986). *Isadora—Portrait of the Artist as a Woman.* New York: McGraw-Hill.

Borchers, K. K. (1985). Do gains made in art therapy persist? A study with aftercare patients. *Amer. Journal of Art Therapy, 23*, 89–91.

Borgmann, A. (1987). The question of Heidegger and technology. *Philosophy Today, 31*, 2–4.

Bowers, J. J. (1992). Therapy through art: Facilitating treatment of sexual abuse. *Journal of Psychosocial Nursing and Mental Health Sciences, 30*(6), 34–35.

Bray, J. D. (1989). The relationships of creativity, time experience

and mystical experience. New York University: CINAHL Abstract.
Brewer, J. F. (1998). Healing sounds. *Complement. Ther. Nurs. Midwif.* 4(1), 7–12.
Burgess, A. W., & Hartman, C. R. (1993). Children's drawings. *Child Abuse and Neglect, 17*(1), 161–168.
Busuttil, J. (1990). An art therapy exhibition: A retrospective view. *British Journal of Occupational Therapy, 53*(12), 501–503.
Campbell, D., & Stanley, J. (1963). *Experimental and quasi-experimental designs for research.* Boston: Houghton Mifflin.
Campbell, J. (1989). *The power of myth—A mystic fire video* [Videotape]. New York: Parabola Magazine.
Camus, A. (1985). *The myth of sisyphus and other essays.* New York: Vintage Books.
Camus, A. (1986). *The plague.* New York: Random House.
Capacchione, L. (1988). *The power of your other hand.* North Hollywood, CA: Newcastle.
Carlisle, D. (1991). Special effects: Arts in health care. *Nursing Times, 87*(46), 50–52.
Carper, B. A. (1978). Fundamental patterns of knowing in nursing. *Advances in Nursing Science, 1*(1), 13–23.
Cheney, S. (1928). *Isadora Duncan—The Art of the Dance.* New York: Theatre Arts Books.
Chinn, P. L. (1985). Debunking myths in nursing theory and research. *Image: The Journal of Scholarly Inquiry, 17*(2), 45–49.
Chinn, P. L. (1989). Nursing patterns of knowing and feminist thought. *Nursing & Health Care, 10*(2), 71–75.
Chinn, P. L. (1991). *A phenomenologic/hermeneutic study of the art of nursing: Experiential interpretive criticism as method.* Proposal-in-progress, February 2.
Chinn, P.L. (1994). *Anthology of art and aesthetics in nursing.* New York: National League for Nursing.
Chinn, P. L., & Kramer, M. (1991). *Theory and nursing: A systematic approach* (3rd ed.). St. Louis: C. V. Mosby.
Chisholm, R. M. (ed.). (1960). *Realism and the background of phenomenology.* New York: The Free Press.
Chlan, L. (1998). Effectiveness of a music therapy intervention on

relaxation and anxiety for patients receiving ventilatory assistance. *Heart Lung, 27*(3), 169–176.

Coles, R. (1990). *The spiritual life of children.* Boston: Houghton Mifflin.

Cooper, J. (1991). What's it worth? Art project in a nursing home. *Nursing Times, 87*(48), 34–35.

Csikszentmihalyi, M. (1990). *Flow.* New York: Harper & Row.

Denzin, N. (1989). *Interpretive Biography Qualitative Research Method Series.* Newbury Park, CA: Sage.

Derrida, J. (1992). *The gift of death.* Chicago: University of Chicago Press.

Dillard, A. (1982). *Pilgrim at tinker creek.* New York: Bantam Books.

Edwards, B. (1986). *Drawing on the artist within.* New York: Simon & Schuster.

Ezzone, S.; Baker, C.; Rosselet, R.; & Terepka, E. (1998). Music as an adjunct to antiemetic therapy. *Oncology Nursing Forum, 25*(9), 1551–1556.

Falco, R. (1989). The people who nurse people with AIDS: A photo essay. *RN, 52*(12), 41–48.

Fawcett, J. (1989). *Analysis and evaluation of conceptual models of nursing* (2nd ed.). Philadelphia: F. A. Davis.

Foucault, M. (1982). *This is not a pipe.* Berkeley: University of California Press.

Gablik. S. (1992). *The re-enchantment of art.* New York: Thames and Hudson.

Gadamer, H. G. (1975). *Truth and method.* New York: Seabury.

Gadow, S. (1980a). Body and self: A dialectic. *Journal of Medicine and Philosophy, 5,* 172–185.

Gadow, S. (1980b). Existential advocacy: Philosophical foundation of nursing. In S. Spicker & S. Gadow (eds.), *Nursing: Images and ideals, opening dialogue with the humanities.* New York: Springer-Verlag.

Gadow, S. (1984). Touch and technology: Two paradigms of patient care. *Journal of Religion and Health, 23*(1).

Gadow, S. (1990). Covenant without cure: Letting go and holding on in chronic illness. In J. Watson & M. Ray (Eds.), *The ethics of care and the ethics of cure: Synthesis and chronicity.* New York: National League for Nursing.

Gadow, S. (1993, April). *Women's health care: Social, medical, and ethical narratives.* Paper presented to the conference on Women, Health Care, and Ethics. University of Tennessee, Knoxville, TN.

Gardner, H. (1982). *Art, mind and brain. A cognitive approach to creativity.* New York: Basic Books.

Gaut, D., & Leininger, M. (1991). *Caring: The compassionate healer.* New York: National League for Nursing.

Gaze, H. (1991). Lessons in creativity: Arts course for carers. *Nursing Times, 87*(34), 54–55.

Ghiselin, B. (1953). *The creative process—A symposium.* Berkeley, CA: University of California Press.

Gillespie, M. A., & Strong, T. B. (1988). *Nietzsche's New Seas. Explorations in philosophy, aesthetics and politics.* Chicago: University of Chicago Press.

Glaister, J. A., & McGuinness, T. (1992). The art of therapeutic drawing: Helping chronic trauma survivors. *Journal of Psychosocial Nursing and Mental Health Sciences, 30*(5), 9–17.

Graham-Pole, J.; Lane, M. T. R.; & Rodriguez, R. (1992). *Art in the bone marrow transplant unit.* Proposal for Children's Miracle Network Grant.

Green, B. L. (1987). Group art therapy as an adjunct to treatment for chronic outpatients. *Hospital and Community Psychiatry, 38,* 988–991.

Grossman, R. (1994). *Phenomenology and existentialism: An introduction.* London, England: Routledge and Kegan Paul.

Gubrium, J. F. (1992). *Out of control family therapy and domestic disorder.* Newbury Park, CA: Sage.

Gubrium, J. F. (1993). *Speaking of life: Horizons of meaning for nursing home residents.* Hawthorne, NY: Aldine De Gruyter.

Gubrium, J. F., & Holstein, J. (1994). *The active interview.* Newbury Park, CA: Sage.

Guess, R. (1981). *The idea of a critical theory: Habermas and the Frankfurt School.* Cambridge: Cambridge University Press.

Hagedorn, M. (1990). Using photography with families of chronically ill children. In M. Leininger (ed.), *The caring imperative in education.* New York: National League for Nursing—Center of Human Caring.

Hagood, M. M. (1991). Group art therapy with mothers of sexually abused children. *Art in Psychotherapy, 18*, 17–24.

Harper, D. (1993). On the authority of the image: Visual methods at the crossroads. *Qualitative Research, 25*, 403–412.

Harvey, Andrew. (1994). *The way of passion: A celebration of rumi.* Berkeley, CA: Frog.

Heidegger, M. (1977). *Basic writings.* New York: Harper & Row.

Heider, K. (1976). *Ethnographic film.* Austin: University of Texas Press.

Heitz, L. (1992). Effect of music therapy in the post-anesthesia care unit. *Journal of Post Anesthesia Nursing, 7*, 22–31.

Highley, B., & Ferentz, T. (1988). *Esoteric inquiry.* New York: National League for Nursing.

Holstein, James A. (1993). *Court-ordered insanity interpretive practice and involuntary commitment.* Hawthorne, NY: Aldine De Gruyter.

Huckabay, L. (1987). The effect on bonding behavior of giving a mother her premature baby's picture. *Scholarly Inquiry for Nursing Practice, 1*(2), 115–129.

Hurley, F. J. (1972). *Portrait of a decade.* Baton Rouge: Louisiana State University Press.

Husserl, E. (1980). *Realism and the background of phenomenology.* New York: The Free Press.

Irwin, H. J. (1991). The depiction of loss: Use of clients' drawings in bereavement counseling. *Death Studies, 15*(5), 481–497.

Jevne, R. (1992). Qualitative research for the dedicated novice. Proceedings of the 4th International Conference on the Psychology of Health, Immunity, and Research of the National Institute for Clinical Application of Behavioral Medicine, New York.

Josselson, R., & Lieblich, A. (1993). *The narrative study of lives.* Newbury Park, CA: Sage.

Kandinsky, W. (1977). *Concerning the spiritual in art.* Translated and with an introduction by M. T. H. Sadler. New York: Dover.

Kelley, S. J. (1984). The use of art therapy with sexually abused children. *Journal of Psychosocial Nursing, 22*(12), 12–18.

Kelley, S. J. (1985). Drawings: Critical communications for sexually abused children. *Pediatric Nursing, 11*(6), 421–426.

Kestenbaum, V. (1982). *The humanity of the ill: Phenomenological perspective.* Knoxville: University of Tennessee Press.

Kierkegaard, S. (1992). *Either/Or, A fragment of life*. London: Penguin.

Kuntz, B. (1991). Exploring the grief of adolescents after the death of a parent. *Journal of Child and Adolescent Psychiatric and Mental Health Nursing, 4*(3), 105–109.

Lane, M. R. (1994). Model of creativity. In P. Chinn (ed.), *Art and aesthetics in nursing*. New York: National League for Nursing.

Lane, M. R. (1998). *Creative Healing*. San Francisco: Harper.

Lane, M. R., and Graham-Pole, J. (1994). Development of an art program on a bone marrow transplant unit. *Cancer Nursing 17*(3), 185–192.

Lane, M. R., and Samuels, M. (1996). Art as a way of healing. In W. Jonas (ed.), *Complementary Textbook of Therapy*. New York: Wiley.

Langeveld, M. J. (1975). *Personal help for children growing up*. London: University of Exeter Press.

Langeveld, M. J. (1983). The stillness of the secret place. *Phenomenology & Pedagogy, 2*(3), 148.

Lazarus, A. (1980). *The practice of multimodel theory*. New York: McGraw-Hill.

LeGuin, U. (1989). *Dancing at the edge of the world: Thoughts on words, women, places*. New York: Harper & Row.

Leibovitz, A. (1992). *Dancers—Photographs by Annie Leibovitz*. Washington, DC: Smithsonian Institution Press.

Levinas, E. (1985). *Ethics and infinity*. Pittsburgh, PA: Duquesne University Press.

Levine, S. K. (1992). *Poeisis*. Toronto: Palmerston Press.

Linschoten, J. (1952). On falling asleep. *Tijdschrift voor Philosophie, 14*, 207–267.

Linschoten, J. (1969). *Aspects of the sexual incarnation: An inquiry concerning the meaning of the body in the sexual encounter*. Utrecht: Bijleveld.

Lyotard, M. (1990). *The postmodern condition: Report on knowledge*. Minneapolis: University of Minnesota Press.

MacDougall, S. (1991). *Whose story is it? Visual anthropology*. New York: Harwood.

McGarry, T. J., & Prince, M. (1998). Implementation of groups for creative expression on a psychiatric unit. *Journal of Psychiatric Nursing Mental Health Services 36*(3), 19–24.

McIntyre, B. B. (1990a). Art therapy with bereaved youth. *Journal of Palliative Care, 6,* 16–25.
McIntyre, B. B. (1990b). An art therapy group for bereaved youth in hospice care. *Caring, 9*(9), 56–58.
McKenzie, B. A. (1998). The art of survival: Unleashing the talents of end stage renal disease patients to increase their wellness. *Journal of Canadian Nursing, 8*(3), 33–35.
McMillan, I. (1991). Art's delight: Creating works of art, impact on people with learning disabilities. *Nursing Times, 87*(36), 52–53.
Merleau-Ponty, M. (1962). *Phenomenology of perception.* London: Routledge and Kegan Paul.
Newman, M. (1986). *Health as expanding consciousness.* St. Louis, MO: C. V. Mosby.
Nietzsche, F. (1961). *Thus spoke Zarathustra.* New York: Penguin.
Nussbaum, M. (1990). *Love's knowledge: Essays on philosophy and literature.* New York: Oxford University Press.
Olive, J. S. (1991). Development of group interpersonal skills through art therapy. *Maladjustment and Therapeutic Education, 9,* 174–180.
Olson, S. L. (1998). Bedside musical care: Applications in pregnancy, childbirth, and neontal care. *Journal of Obstet. Gynecol. Neonatal Nursing 27*(5), 569–575.
Pacchetti, C.; Aglieri, R.; Mancini, F.; Martignoni, E.; & Nappi, G. (1998). Active music therapy and Parkinson's disease: Methods. *Funt. Neurol. 13*(1), 57–67.
Pennebaker, J. W. (1987). The psychophysiology of confession: Linking inhibitory and psychosomatic process. *Journal of Personality and Psychosomatic Process, 52,* 781–793.
Polit, D., & Hungler, B. (1991). *Nursing research principles and methods* (4th ed.). Philadelphia: Lippincott.
Polkinghorne, D. (1983). *Methodology for the human science: Systems of inquiry.* Albany, NY: State University of New York Press.
Predeger, E. (1996). Womanspirit: A journey into healing through art in breast cancer. *Adv. Nurs. Sci. 18*(3), 48–58.
Radziewicz, R. M., & Schneider, S. M. (1992). Using diversional activity to enhance coping. *Cancer Nursing, 15*(4), 293–298.
Reissman, Catherine Kohler. (1993). *Narrative analysis qualitative research methods series.* Newbury Park, CA: Sage.

Rollins, J. H. (1990). The arts: Helping children cope with hospitalization. *Imprint, 37*(4), 79–83.

Romero, R. (1986). Autobiographical scrapbooks: A coping tool for hospitalized school children. *Issues in Comprehensive Pediatric Nursing, 9*(4), 247–258.

Russ, S. (1993). *Affect and creativity: The role of affect and play in the creative process.* Trenton, NJ: Erlbaum.

Samuels, M. (1990). *Art as a healing force: Essay.* New York: Bolinas Museum.

Sandelowski, Margarete. (1993). On the aesthetics of qualitative research image. *Journal of Nursing Scholarship, 27*(3).

Sarter, B. (1988). Innovative research methods for nursing. *Omery Ethnography,* 17–31.

Sartre, J. P. (1988). *Being and nothingness.* New York: Pocket Books.

Savedra, M., & Highley, B. L. (1988). Photography: Is it useful in learning how adolescents view hospitalization? *Journal of Adolescent Health Care, 9*(3), 219–222.

Shapiro, B. (1985). All I have is pain: Art therapy in an inpatient chronic pain relief unit. *American Journal of Art Therapy, 24,* 44–48.

Shilma, L. (1984). Portraits. *Phenomenology & Pedagogy, 2*(3), 211.

Sourkes, B. M. (1991). Truth to life: Art therapy with pediatric oncology patients and their siblings. *Journal of Psychosocial Oncology, 9*(2), 81–96.

Stern, R. S. (1989). Many ways to grow: Creative art therapies. *Pediatric Annals, 645,* 649–652.

Stotts, R. C., & Pickett, J. (1987). The camera as a nursing tool: Photography in a nursing home. *Geriatric Nursing, American Journal of Care for the Aging, 8*(3), 130–132.

Street, A. F. (1992). *A critical ethnography of clinical nursing.* Albany, NY: State University of New York Press.

Tibbetts, T. J. (1990). The creative art therapies with adolescents. *Arts in Psychotherapy, 17,* 139–146.

Updike, P. A. (1990a). Music therapy results for ICU patients. *Dimensions of Critical Care Nursing, 9,* 39–45.

Updike, P. A. (1990b). Through the lens of the artist-scientist: Reflections for the pediatric oncology nurse. *Journal of Pediatric Oncology Nursing, 7*(1), 4–8.

REFERENCES

Updike, P. A. (1998). Opening to the sacred: Intentional use of music to engage the spiritual dimension. *Adv. Prac. Nurs. Q. 4*(1), 64–69.

Van den Berg, J. H. (1970). *Things: Four metabolic reflections.* Pittsburgh, PA: Duquesne University Press.

Van Manen, M. (1990). *Researching the lived experience.* Washington, DC: Human Science for an Action Sensitive Pedagogy.

Van Manen, M. (1995). On the epistemology of reflective practice. *Teachers & Teaching: Theory & Practice, 1*(1), 45.

Villarruel, A. M., and Denyes, M. J. (1991). Pain assessment in children: Theoretical and empirical validity. *Advances in Nursing Science, 14*(2), 32–41.

Walker, C. (1989). Use of art and play therapy in pediatric oncology. *Journal of Pediatric Oncology Nursing, 6*(4), 121–126.

Walsh, J. (1991). *Future images: An art intervention with suicidal adolescents.* Unpublished dissertation, University of South Carolina, Raleigh.

Watson, C. (1987). Portrait study: Dehumanization of patients in an intensive care unit—Having a photograph. *Nursing Times, 83*(25), 24–30.

Watson, J. (1988). *Nursing: Human science and human care, a theory for nursing.* New York: National League for Nursing.

Watson, J. (1990). Caring knowledge and informed moral passion. *Advances in Nursing Science, 14*(11), 111–121.

Watson, J. (1993). Personal communication. May 15, 1993.

Weinberg, D. J. (1985). The potential for computer art therapy for cerebrovascular accident and brain trauma patients. *Art Therapy, 2,* 66–72.

White, J. M. (1992). Music therapy: An intervention to reduce anxiety in the myocardial infarction patient. *Clinical Nurse Specialist, 6,* 58–63.

Williams, H. (1984). *Notes for a young painter.* Englewood Cliffs, NJ: Prentice Hall.

Williams, H. (1989). *Art/Life.* Unpublished manuscript. Gainesville, FL. Referenced from Young's manuscript.

Willis, Paul. (1990). *Common culture. Symbolic work at play in the everyday cultures of the young.* Boulder, CO: Westview Press.

Ziller, R. (1990). *Photographing the self.* Newbury Park, CA: Sage.

Zimmerman, M. L.; Wolbert, W. A.; Burgess, A. W.; and Hartman, C. R. (1987). Art and group work: Interventions for multiple victims of child molestation. Part 2. *Archives of Psychiatric Nursing, 1*(1), 40–46.

Zukav, G. (1989). *The seat of the soul.* New York: Simon & Schuster.

Resources

Academy for Guided Imagery, Inc.
P.O. Box 2070
Mill Valley, CA 94942

American Holistic Health Association
P.O. Box 17400
Anaheim, CA 92817–7400
(714) 779–6152

Institute of Noetic Sciences
475 Gate Five Road, Suite #300
Sausalito, CA 94965
Fax: (415) 331–5673

American Holistic Nurses' Association
(800) 278–AHNA
E-mail: AHNA-Conference@flaglink.com
Web: *http://ahna.org/*

NICABM
P.O. Box 523
Mansfield, CT 06250
(800) 743–2226 or (860) 456–1153

Fax: (860) 423–4512
E-mail: *nicabm@neca.com*

American Holistic Medical Association
(703) 556–9245
Fax: (703) 556–8729

Association for Transpersonal Psychology
P.O. Box 3049
Stanford, CA 94309
(415) 863–9941

Alternative Therapies
P.O. Box 17969
Durham, NC 27715
2400 Pratt Street Durham, NC 27705
(919) 668–8825
Fax: (919) 668–7046
E-mail: *ATEditors@onyx.dcri.duke.edu*

Web sites for spiritual healing links

Max Van Manen, phenomenology, method
http://www.ualberta. ca/~vanmanen/mvm/vanmanen.htm

Vigili web site world wheel
http://www.arcosanti.org/people/ wheel.html

Alternative medicine links
http://www.altmedicine.com/app/registeruser.cfm
http://www.siu.edu/departments/ bushea/altmed.html

Spiritual development and holistic medicine
http://www.holisticmed.com/www/spirit.html

Holistic healing link
http://www.holisticmed.com/www/www.html

Index

adrenal glands, 31
adrenaline, 30, 31
aesthetic inquiry, xiii
affirmations, 117
  for embodying the spirit, 204
  for experiencing transcendence, 213
  for feeling energy and compassion, 207
  for going elsewhere, 188–89
  for knowing the truth and trusting the process, 201
  for pain and darkness, 185
  for slipping through the veil, 197
  for the turning point, 195–96
afterlife, belief in, 33
AIDS patients, 10
  mind-body techniques used by, 27
  stories of, 103–104
alcoholism, 141–43
angels:
  dancing with, xv–xvi, 165–67
  glimpsing, 2, 111–12, 153, 163–65, 210–11
arousal/release cycle, 30
arthritis, 112, 161–62

Artist's Way, The (Cameron), 191
arts, healing through the, xi–xii, 1, 60, 88–89, 88–92, 114–15, 168–69, 170, 187, 189–91, 192–93
  basket making, 21–22, 193
  body castings, 92
  drawing, 65–66, 89–90, 104–105, 113–14, 164–65
  guided imagery to find your artist within, 96–97
  parasympathetic nervous system and, 30
  physiological effects of, 27, 29
  resolving opposites, 88
  sculpture, 45, 46, 90–91
attention, *see* concentration
autonomic nervous system, 29–30
  parasympathetic branch of, 30, 31, 106
  sympathetic branch of, 30
awareness, cultivating, 204

basket making, 21–22, 193
  see also arts, healing through the
Benson, Herbert, 29, 106

INDEX

black humor, 143
Blessed Mother, visions of, 160, 211
blood flow:
    autonomic nervous system and, 29, 30
    optimizing, 3, 27, 31
blood pressure, lowering of, 29, 30, 31
body castings, 92
    see also arts, healing through the
body sensations:
    concentration on, 205, 206–207
    of healing energy, 144
Bolen, Jean Shinoda, 43, 60
books used in healing, 43, 60, 191–92, 197
boundaries, letting down your, 205–206
breathing exercises, 182, 206
breathing rate:
    autonomic nervous system and, 30
    lowering the, 29, 30, 31
    synchronization of, 105, 106
Buddha of Compassion, 146–47

Cameron, Julia, 191
cancer patients, 2, 10, 112
    mind-body techniques used by, 27
    poetry of, 159
    resolution of life and death through art, 88
    stories of, xv–xvi, 7–10, 37–39, 78–80, 90–91, 93, 99–100, 111–12, 115–16, 123–27, 131–32, 137–40, 144–45, 151–53, 155–57, 165–67
    support groups, beneficial effects of, 32–33
caregiver's pain, 43–44
Christ:
    embodiment of pure spirit, 127
    seeing, 161–62
coincidence, watching for, 187
collective consciousness, 34, 68
compassion, *see* healing energy of love and compassion, feeling the
concentration, 29, 41, 184–85
    slipping through the veil and, 104–106
connectedness, feelings of, 29
Creative Healing (Lane and Samuels), xv, 1, 191
creativity, 190
    the arts, *see* arts, healing through the
    emergence of creative spirit, 81–82
    healing and creative process, 80–81
    as long-term process, 92–93
    parasympathetic nervous system and, 30
    unconscious and, 82
crisis, teachings from people in, xv–xvi
"Crossing the Beckoning Threshold," 159
Cut Out My Heart, 50

Dalai Lama, 127
dance, 69, 85–88, 103–104, 141, 195
    with angels, xv–xvi, 165–67
dancing on one foot, metaphor of, 117
darkness, *see* pain and darkness
Darshan, 125, 127, 169
daydreaming, 71, 186
depression, xi–xii, 2, 10, 21–22, 63, 69–70, 90, 94, 112
drawing, 65–66, 89–90, 104–105, 113–14, 164–65
    see also arts, healing through the
dreams, 186
    going elsewhere with, 62–63
    pain and darkness and, 46–47, 48–49, 50
    seeing Christ in, 161, 162
dying:
    fear of, talking about your, 184
    transcendence, *see* transcendence

Earth, healing the, 94–95, 167–69
ecstasy of transcendence, 154
embodiment of the spirit, 23, 123–36
    affirmations for, 204
    being the love that you are, 133, 134–35
    expecting nothing in return, 133

INDEX

guided imagery, 134–36
near death, 127, 133
prescriptions for, 201–204
reflections on, 132
stories of, 123–27, 128–30
viewing life from new perspective, 131
enchantment:
illuminosity and, 157–58
slipping through the veil to place of, 100–102
endorphins, 32
energy, healing, 34
see also healing energy of love and compassion, feeling the
enlightenment, experience of, 196
epinephrine (adrenaline), 31
extraction of pain, 49–50, 184

faith, 13–14
Fawzy, UCLA study of role of support in longevity of melanoma patients by, 32–33
fears, facing your, 44–46, 184
fibromyalgia patients, 89–90
"fight or flight" response, 30
focusing, 113

gardens and gardening, 93
God:
belief in, 33
experiencing, 2, 7–10, 153–54, 159, 210
going elsewhere, 23, 51–76
acting on the invitation to heal, 67
affirmations for, 188–89
daydreaming, 71, 186, 187
feeling safe and protected, 71
going inward into your heart, 64
guided imagery, 72–76
inviting the pause, 71
opening your heart, 68
the pause that invites and, 62
prescriptions for, 185–89
reflections on, 70
restory your own life, 61–62

shutting off what upsets you, 188
stories of, 59–60, 62–63, 64–66, 68–70
the trigger event, 66–68, 72, 187
Grey, Alex, 158, 209
grief, dealing with, 34, 44, 84–85
guided imagery, 1, 3, 27, 191
for embodiment of the spirit, 134–36
to experience the light of the essence of healing, 17–18
to feel healing energy of love and compassion, 147–50
to find your turning point, 96–97
for going elsewhere, 72–76
history of, 13
for knowing the truth and trusting the process, 119–21
pain and darkness, to emerge from, 52–58
purpose of, 13
for slipping through the veil, 107–109
spirit illumination, 14–16
for transcendence, 170–77
universal spirit, seeing your, 17

Halifax, Joan, 42
hallucination, inviting a, 208
healing circle, 195
healing energy of love and compassion, feeling the, 24, 34, 137–50, 204–207
affirmations for, 207
ancient concept of healing energy, 141
body sensations of, 144
Buddha of Compassion exercise, 146–47
exercise to increase feelings of compassion, 146–47
the experience of, 140, 144
guided imagery, 147–50
humor and, 143
letting go, 141
prescriptions for, 205–207
pure compassion, 146

249

healing energy of love and compassion, feeling the (*cont.*)
   reflections on, 146–47
   seeing energy, 144
   stories of, 141–43, 144–45
heart disease, patients with, 2, 10, 29
heart rate:
   autonomic nervous system and, 29–30
   lowering of, 29, 30, 31
hermeneutic method, xiii
Hindu religion, 34
hormonal system, 27
   spiritual change and, 30
House of God, The, 143
humor, 143
hypothalamus, 29, 30, 31

illumination of the spirit, 12, 19
   guided imagery to see, 14–16
illuminosity, xiv, 154–59
imagery:
   physiological response to spiritual, *see* physiology of Spirit Body Healing
   spiritual experience perceived as, 28, 157
imagination, using your, 186–87
immune system, 3, 27
   spiritneuroimmunology, 31–32
impatience, 199
interconnectedness, 158
International Transformative Arts, 114

journals, 47, 83–84, 91, 132, 187
judgment, stopping, 206
Jung, Carl, 33

knowing the truth and trusting the process, 23, 111–21
   affirmations for, 201
   compared to flowing like a river, 113
   dancing on one foot, metaphor of, 117
   experience of knowing the truth, 112
   finding meaning in your own life story, 118
   the first insight, 116
   going with the flow, 118
   guided imagery, 119–21
   letting go of negativity, 119
   prescriptions for, 198–201
   reflections on, 116–17
   revelations, 115–16
   spontaneous insights, 113–14
   stories of, 111–12, 113–16
   surrendering, 113

Lane, Mary Rockwood:
   Creative Healing, xv, 1, 191
   healing through painting, personal experience of, xi–xii, 49–50, 116
   research study on how the spirit heals, xii–xvi
longevity and spiritual healing, 32–33
love:
   beneath the pain, 114–15
   embodiment of the spirit and, 133, 134–35
   healing energy of, *see* healing energy of love and compassion, feeling the
   sharing in transcendence, 154

mandala, 41
mantras, 193
meditation, 1, 27, 106, 191, 219–21
   learning to meditate, 182–83
   physiology of, 29
memories:
   pain and darkness and, 46, 49, 50
   of spiritual experiences, honoring, 197
merging, 209
   embodiment of your spirit and, 201, 203
   slipping through the veil likened to, 101, 106–107
mind-body techniques, 1, 2–4
   research into physical effects of, 27

see also specific techniques, e.g. guided imagery; relaxation
mindful present, 210
mind's eye, seeing through the, *see* guided imagery
Montgomery-Whicher, Rose, 89
"Mourning Sickness," 85
Moving Point of Balance, 114
music, 184

nature, 94–95, 167–69, 186, 190, 192, 209
negativity, letting go of, 119
neurotransmitters, 27, 31–32

Ornish, Dean, 29, 33

pain and darkness, xiv, 22–23, 37–58
  affirmations for, 185
  books as tools to start the journey, 44
  as doorway to Spirit Body healing, 39–40
  dreams and memories from the past, 46–49, 50
  externalizing, 50
  extraction of pain, 49–50, 184
  facing fear, 44–46
  facing your pain, 183
  fear of, 184
  guided imagery, 52–58
  inviting the light, 51–52
  knowing healing begins with, 50
  looking for a glimmer in, 51
  prescriptions for, 182–85
  reflections on, 50
  restorying your illness, 183–84
  stories of, 37–46, 48–49
painting, *see* arts, healing through the
parasympathetic nervous system, 30, 31, 106
pelvic inflammatory disease, story of patient with, 40–41
phenomenological study, xiii
physiology of Spirit Body Healing, 27–34

hormonal system changes, 31
longevity and spirit, 32–33
nervous system changes, 29–30
spiritneuroimmunology, 31–32
spiritual visions, healing with, 28–29
Pilgrimages (Bolen), 43, 60
pilgrimage to a sacred site, 193–94
poetry, 44, 47, 77, 84–85, 159
popes, 127
prayer, 47, 132, 170, 194, 210
  embodied, spiritual work as, 208
  parasympathetic nervous system and, 30
  physiology of, 29
  release of endorphins during, 32
  research on, 27, 33
prescriptions for Spirit Body Healing, 181–213
  for embodying your spirit, 201–204
  for experiencing transcendence, 208–13
  for feeling the healing energy of love and compassion, 205–207
  for finding your turning point, 189–96
  for going elsewhere, 185–89
  how to use, 181
  for knowing the truth and trusting the process, 198–201
  for pain and darkness, 181–85
  for slipping through the veil, 196–97
psychoneuroimmunology, 32

reflections as teaching tools, 12–13
relationship problems, 10, 47, 128–9
relationships, healing and, 33–34
relaxation, 1, 27, 31
  parasympathetic nervous system and, 30
  physiology of, 29
relaxation response, 106
Relaxation Response, The (Benson), 29
Remen, Rachel, 125
restory your own life, 24–25, 61–62, 146, 183–84

251

INDEX

rituals:
  creating, 187
  planning your own healing, 194–95
rivers, healing and saving, 94–95
Roualt, Georges, 88

sacred space discovered with Spirit Body Healing, 169
Samuels, Michael, 1–4, 123–27
  Creative Healing, xv, 1, 191
  Seeing with the Mind's Eye, 3
Samuels, Nancy, 123–27, 132
sculpture, 45, 46, 90–91
  see also arts, healing through the
Seeing with the Mind's Eye (Samuels), 3
sexual abuse, 64–66
Shamanic Voices (Halifax), 42
shamanism, 42, 43, 51, 60–61, 195
  defined, 51
  initiation rites, 66
slipping through the veil, 23, 99–101
  affirmations for, 197
  described, 100–101
  enchantment, to place of, 100, 102
  guided imagery, 107–109
  likened to merging, 101, 106–107
  prescriptions for, 196–97
  riveting attention and, 104–105
  to spaciousness, 101–102
  stories of, 99–100, 103–104
Spiegel, David, 32
spirit, embodiment of the, *see* embodiment of the spirit
Spirit Body Healing:
  "doing right action in the world" and, 11, 70, 212
  eight steps of, xiv, 22–24, 181
  to help recover from life-threatening illnesses and crises, 10–11
  physiology of, *see* physiology of Spirit Body Healing
  prescriptions for, *see* prescriptions for Spirit Body Healing
  the process of, 21–25

research study, xii–xvi, 1
sacred space of, 169
shift in consciousness, xiv
as spiraling process, 22, 101, 130, 181
step 1: pain and darkness, *see* pain and darkness
step 2: going elsewhere, *see* going elsewhere
step 3: the turning point, *see* turning point, finding your
step 4: slipping through the veil, *see* slipping through the veil
step 5: embodiment of the spirit, *see* embodiment of the spirit
step 6: knowing the truth and trusting the process, *see* knowing the truth and trusting the process
step 7: healing energy and compassion, *see* healing energy of love and compassion, feeling the
step 8: transcendence, *see* transcendence, experiencing
spiritneuroimmunology, 31–32
spiritual history, taking an inventory of your, 196–97
spiritual visions, 33
  in history, 28
  parasympathetic nervous system and, 30
  physiological changes accompanying, 28–29
  release of endorphins during, 32
Stanford University, 32
stories:
  of embodiment of the spirit, 123–27, 128–30
  of feeling the healing energy of love and compassion, 141–43, 144–45
  of finding your turning point, 78–80, 83–85, 88–89, 94–95
  of going elsewhere, 59–60, 62–63, 64–66, 68–70
  of knowing the truth and trusting the process, 111–12, 113–16
  of pain and darkness, 37–46, 48–49

peak spiritual experience common to all, 25
purpose of the, 12–13
restory your own life, 24–25, 61–62, 146, 183–84
of slipping through the veil, 99–100, 103–104
of transcendence, 151–53, 155–57, 158, 160, 161–67, 168–69
stress hormones, 30
stress reduction, 29
support groups, 32–33, 34
surrendering, 113
Swartz, Beth Ames, 114
sympathetic nervous system, 30

T cells, 32
teachings from the edge, 215–18
Tiger Woman (sculpture), 45, 46
transcendence, experiencing, xiv, xvi, 11, 24, 151–77
　affirmations for, 213
　Blessed Mother, visions of the, 160, 211
　dancing with angels, 165–67
　ecstasy of, 154
　enchantment, 157–58
　feelings of oneness, 153
　glimpsing angels, 153, 163–65, 210–11
　guided imagery, 170–77
　healing the Earth, 167–69
　illuminosity and, 154–59
　interconnectedness and, 158
　moving to a place focused on others, 167–68
　prescriptions for experiencing, 208–13
　quieting down to hear the voices of the spirit, 212
　reflections on, 169–70
　seeing Christ, 161–62
　seeing yourself as surrounded by God and angels, 153–54
　seeing yourself for the first time, 154
　sharing love, 154
　stories of, 151–53, 155–57, 158, 160, 161–67, 168–69
trigger events for going elsewhere, 66–68, 72, 187
truth, knowing the, *see* knowing the truth and trusting the process
turning point, finding your, 23, 77–97
　affirmations for, 195–96
　with art, 88–92, 189–91, 192–93
　through creativity, 80–82, 93–94, 190
　with dance, 85–88
　in gardens, 93
　guided image for, 96–97
　with journaling, 83–84
　openness of mind and, 82–83
　prescriptions for, 189–96
　reflections on, 95–96
　stories of, 78–80, 83–85, 88–89, 94–95

unconscious, healing images from the, 82
universal spirit, 11, 17
University of Florida research study on healing through creativity, xii–xvi, 1

water, connecting with, 184–85